THE
MOTHERHOOD
RESET

Vibrant Mamas Series

THE MOTHERHOOD RESET

A Clinical Psychologist's Guide to Finding
Calm, Confidence and Contentment in Motherhood

DR HILARY CLAIRE ROWSELL

Books by Dr Hilary Claire Rowsell

The Motherhood Reset: A Clinical Psychologist's Guide to Finding Calm, Confidence and Contentment in Motherhood

Nourished Mama Roadmap: A Clinical Psychologist's Guide to Abundant Energy in Motherhood

Mama, Let It Go: A Clinical Psychologist's Guide to Finding Joy, Freedom and Ease in Motherhood

DEDICATION

This book is dedicated to my two little munchkins, for without you, I would never have gone on the wild and wonderful adventure that is motherhood.

CONTENTS

INTRODUCTION

Let's start with what this book is not

This is <u>not</u> another book telling you that the secret to happiness in motherhood is a mysterious balance of bubble baths, getting your nails done and indulging in some chocolate or wine. If that were the answer to feeling overwhelmed and burnt out, you wouldn't be looking for a book about motherhood in the first place.

This book is <u>not</u> about disguising superficial selfcare as the cure for all your worries and exhaustion. It won't vaguely tell you how to "do it all" and give empty advice like "get a massage" before sending you back to a lifestyle where you're stressed 99% of the time. We all know that doesn't address the deeper issues at play.

What modern day moms do need, what *you* need, is true selfcare, the kind that occurs when you are connected to your purpose, wellbeing and self. It is not being that stereotypical selfless, compliant, mother figure who loses her identity outside of her children and then treats herself once in a while to fulfilling her basic needs and calling it a luxury.

It isn't about telling you what motherhood should look like. This is about what you want it to look like.

This book is a roadmap with tangible directions and action-able steps to help you live your life as a mother on your terms and your terms alone – whatever those may be! This is a book grounded in psychology and research, written to reclaim your power, your spark, your energy and your health as you set about navigating the ever-challenging terrain that is motherhood.

This book won't be your life-preserver when you feel like you're drowning in motherhood, because it's a clear lesson plan to help you learn how to swim confidently so that you don't drown at all.

This book is the key to becoming the vibrant mama you've always wanted to be.

So, what is a vibrant mama?

She might sound like an impossible dream, a figment of your imagination inspired by unrealistic movies and glamorous online personalities. But guess what? She's not. She is entirely possible – and she's in you already.

While we will all have different specifics of what exactly a vibrant mama is, at her core she is thriving in her version of motherhood – not just surviving. She is calm, content and confident in the uniqueness of her life.

A vibrant mama does motherhood her way, on her own terms. She puts herself first because she knows this is essential for the wellbeing of everyone else – especially her kids. She has clarity about what she wants in her life and about what is most import-ant to her as an individual. She prioritizes her needs without guilt by nourishing her body and mind with good sleep, beautiful food and time in nature. She lets go of the unnecessary. She has traded busyness and exhaustion for a more intentional pace. She focuses her time on what matters most to her.

A vibrant mama doesn't let limiting beliefs and outdated societal expectations about what a "good mom should do" drive her decisions. She *chooses* what type of mother she wants to be and sets her own definition of what motherhood looks like.

She is connected with other moms and gets the support she needs when she needs it. She is bright, present and grateful – and her kids notice this about her. She is at ease, enjoying motherhood even though it innately has its challenges. She is showing up fully as the joyful and serene version of herself. And yet, she also gives herself grace when she has a challenging day.

A vibrant mama creates a meaningful life for herself – not just for her children.

She is within me.

She is within you.

Are you ready to meet her? I'd love to introduce you!

I know how this sounds – this might seem like an impossible dream at the moment, but together we can get there. We can empower the vibrant mama within you, without adding stress to your day-to-day. I know this is possible due to my training, education and research, as a clinical psychologist but more intimately, I know this is possible because this is the journey I went through myself as a mother.

My personal wake up call with motherhood

I'll never forget the day I sat down with my husband, Luke, and we decided to start a family. We always knew we wanted to be parents, but to talk about it made it real. It felt like a momentous adventure to be stepping into motherhood, but I was excited and ready.

I came to Australia from where we both grew up in Canada not long after Luke began medical school in Wollongong. I travelled. I completed my yoga teacher training in the free-spirited, yoga capital, Byron Bay. Shortly after, I found myself starting my Ph.D. in clinical psychology here too. Jobs came up and the opportunity to explore more of the country struck our fancy. We moved from just south of Sydney to the Great Barrier Reef and then onto the rugged and wild outback. Eventually, we settled into a small city on the serene east coast. The years ticked on and suddenly there we were, planning on raising little Aussies.

In my mind, I already knew the kind of mother I was going to be. I was going to be present, energetic and playful with my babies, obviously. We imagined that we would continue to go on all sorts of adventures with our little ones in tow. We didn't just dream but believed we could do it all. We loved the beachy, casual lifestyle we had, our careers and the travel we did – and in our minds, a couple of kiddos weren't going to change that. No biggie, right? How hard could it be? (If only I could go back and tell my younger self what I know now!)

I remember thinking that we could totally handle this parenting thing. I mean, by that point in my life I had been running parenting courses and working therapeutically with parents and kids for years. Luke was a GP who worked extensively with young families. He had even assisted at several births. Caring for our own baby couldn't be that different, could it?

I got pregnant easily and soon I was shopping for the perfect stroller, pretty patterned cloth diapers, a car seat and organic cotton onesies. We decided that Luke would work half days for the first two weeks after our first baby was born and assumed we would manage it all with ease. After all, he was a doctor, I was a psychologist, surely, we were prepared. My pregnancy progressed and then after a long labour, Oak was born ten days before his due date. He was healthy and perfect. The feeling of love I had was infinite. Luke and I were ecstatic and in awe, but...

The struggle is real!

The first few months (let's be honest, the first few years) of motherhood were tough! So much tougher than I could have ever imagined. I had never realized how precious a good night's sleep was before this tiny, squishy little being of my dreams came into my life. I couldn't believe what was happening to me! I found myself struggling with depletion, exhaustion and overwhelm. I certainly wasn't handling anything, let alone "it all," with ease. I was angry with my past self for ever using the word ease in relation to motherhood. I took on too much. I was up several times throughout the night with Oak, attempting to cook beautiful meals every day, fell into an odd obsession of keeping the house pristine, and was trying to be the perfect eco mama. I was even doing online study and creating a new business on the side.

I put impossibly high expectations on myself to do it all, all the time for everyone in the family. I unintentionally put myself last on the priority list. (Confession: I'm not sure I even acknowledged myself as a priority really.)

I was sleep deprived and my normal routines were thrown out the window. I barely showered during those early days. I had to make the choice between getting more sleep or getting a few minutes of me time – and inevitably that "me time" was swallowed up by me picking up toys or writing out grocery lists. Not restful at all. I found it so hard to explain how I was feeling to anyone – even good friends and my husband. I myself wasn't even clear about what I was feeling or what I needed, let alone how to ask others for help. The frustration boiled within. I knew that I should take better care of myself, take time away from the family and do things that were recharging for me, but I was too tired to take that first step.

So, the only thing that could happen, happened – I crashed. Hard. I was depleted of critical nutrients and lacked adequate quality sleep. I later found out I had developed postpartum thyroiditis that completely zapped the vitality, energy and spark out of me.

I was that exhausted and burnt out mom – the one that I was so certain I would never become. And, perhaps the worst part, is that I didn't see it coming.

What happened to me?

I became a classic case of a mom with postnatal depletion that is so prevalent in modern day mamas, only I didn't recognize it at the time. My brain was foggy. Countless times I would walk into a room and completely blank on what I went in there for. I was moody, resentful and the smallest decisions completely overwhelmed me. I lost my ability to do simple math, which perhaps doesn't sound dire, but for someone with a Ph.D. in psychology and a genuine passion for statistics (they are sort of one and the same in that degree), it was devastating. My mind was getting muddled when simply adding up what I was buying from the wholefoods shop. Administrative tasks that used to be a breeze, like applying for passports for Oak, were too overwhelming. I was just surviving each day, a shell of my former self.

Don't get me wrong, there were many moments where I was bursting with love, where I was playful and was having fun. But even in these moments I felt heavy. It was a far cry from the present, fun and lively mom I envisioned for myself when I entered into motherhood. It was as if every little task was a momentous effort.

When Luke would come home after a long day at work, I felt irritated and worn thin, but I couldn't even explain how I was feeling to him. Anything he said was the wrong thing to say. I was snappy and grumpy. Luke would pick up Oak, coo and happily spin him around. When I watched this, I felt ashamed that I wasn't loving every moment with Oak like he was. I desperately wanted to love mothering. While I did love being a mother, doing it 24/7 and much of the time alone was taking a toll – on myself and on my relationship.

I couldn't even remember the last time I had sat on the toilet or showered without a wriggly monkey demanding to be right there with me. How dare Luke get to have breaks from parenting while I was bogged down in the never-ending cycle of soothing, changing, carrying and entertaining our baby. How dare he got to go about furthering his career while mine came to a screeching halt. How dare he all the things, my mind would whisper to me. There was no break for me! It was unfair, so I lashed out.

Sometimes I'd wake up, look in the mirror and think:

"Why is this so hard for me and not for other moms?"

"I am going to break if I keep going like this."

"I just need a rest but then how am I going to take care of Oak and get everything that I need to get done?"

I felt paralyzed – stuck in the struggle.

It was shocking to go from having a busy, challenging career that I had worked toward for years (literally 10 years of higher education to achieve. Bah!) to being home by myself all day, every day with a tiny demanding munchkin and singing nursery rhymes.

I heard a lot of people complain about the diapers that come with babies, but honestly, diaper changing was the easiest part of parenting for me. It was the massive shift in my identity and daily life that viciously clobbered me. The expectations I put on myself, the unrelenting sameness of every day and the exhaustion of doing it all without a support team wore me down. Give me a diaper any day over that!

A shift was needed

One afternoon as I lay on the bed as Oak slept nestled into me, I began daydreaming, as I often did, about what I wished my life looked like. It had become almost a guilty pleasure, imagining an entirely different life than the one I was currently leading.

In my fantasy I was back at the yoga studio. I was getting support from others and not trying to do everything myself. I was spending lots of time with friends and family and less time alone. I had time to focus on my work and I was getting more sleep. I was playful, kind and focused. I was in tune with my needs and found healthy ways to get these met. I was also the girl who gave herself the time to wash her hair regularly and even straighten it once a week (what a luxury!) How had such a normal thing become such a huge act of selfcare in my world?

Something about that day made me realize that I wasn't living a life that was aligned with my values of connection, joy and play. I realized that daydreaming wasn't what I needed – I needed to take action. I needed to build a life that I didn't want to escape from.

That was the day that I decided enough was enough. I made the conscious choice that I was not going to continue like this. I refused to stand back and watch myself become yet another burnt out mom who was just getting by and losing herself in the process (and why is this an accepted stereotypical norm to begin with?!)

So, I dug into research, my training and my experience thus far of motherhood to find a way for me to stop just surviving motherhood and to start thriving in it. How? Don't worry, we'll get into all the details, but broadly speaking:

- I got crystal clear on the type of mom I wanted to be and what was most important in my life. MY life.
- I put myself back at the top of my priority list.
- I made my health and wellness an integral part of daily life.
- I started paying attention to my own needs and emotions – not just my children's.
- I began making decisions from the perspective of my future vibrant self instead of from my current tired reality.
- I took responsibility for my life, choices and wellbeing.
- I let go of the unhelpful and unnecessary expectations, beliefs and identities that were holding me back.
- I sought out connections with others.
- I got clear on what I wanted and took unapologetic action to make motherhood my own.

It didn't happen overnight, but slowly I moved out of the fog. Clarity was where it all started for me. Once I had this clarity, everything got easier. Choices became simpler, which was massive for me since even the smallest decision at the time was bringing me to tears. This flowed into me creating a life that was nourishing me completely and bringing me back to health. Finally, there were several things that I let go of to fully embody who I wanted to be without being weighed down. It felt great!

Where I'm at now – and why I want you to join me

Now not only do I feel confident and full of energy (even with two little kiddos in tow these days!), but I am also more patient, appreciative and present in my life. I can more easily show up as the best version of myself in my relationships, career and as a mom (most of the time, because we're all only human).

I have found a way of living that works for me and my family. Now, there is more joy, space and calm within me and in my life. I want that for you too – and you can have it!

Don't get me wrong, mothering is never going to be effortless. Far from it! But by getting clear on what is most important to you, by prioritizing yourself and by letting go of the unnecessary, you can make it a whole lot easier and more enjoyable for yourself. And when you are thriving, you can show up as a better mother to your kids with a whole lot more ease, for real this time.

It's ironic that for so many of us creating life drains us of our own. But I'm living proof that it doesn't have to be that way – you grew a human life within you, you can nurture and grow the life you want for yourself as well.

Together we can make vibrant and thriving moms the new norm for motherhood!

The first step is clarity

This book will help you move from chaos to calm in motherhood. It will support you in letting go of the things that hold you back from finding joy, peace and energy in your daily life.

It will connect you to what is most important to you and teach you how to shape your life meaningfully around these values. It will guide you in creating your own unique path as a mom.

But in order to do any of that, we have to start with a basic principle – getting clear on what you want. If you don't know where you want to get to, it can be challenging to know what steps to take. You can easily get caught up in other people's expectations and societal pressures, which will then drastically lead you down a path away from what makes you fulfilled and happy.

Clarity brings confidence to your choices. It allows you to know what it is that you need. It also informs what you want to spend your time and energy on. With clarity, no longer will you be at the whim of other people's demands. It will be much easier to live with purpose, enjoy motherhood and step into being your unique version of what a vibrant mama is.

This is what this book is all about – discovering, embracing and activating your clarity.

How to maximize this book as a resource
If I may, I would suggest reading this book once through and complete the strategies within each chapter as you go. Then keep it as a resource for when tricky things come up or you notice yourself slipping back into fatigue and fogginess. We all need a refresher once in a while, especially while trying to create new habits for ourselves. New habits take time and practice. Going from depleted to vibrant takes time and practice too.

As you go through these chapters, have your journal ready. This is your time to explore what you want, what is most important to you and what you want your life to be about. Take notes. Write down ideas that come to mind. Work through the activities at the end of each chapter. Have fun. This will facilitate clarity.

Let's begin

My wish for you is that you find calm, contentment and confidence in motherhood, because it can be one of the most empowering times in our lives. But we all need a little help to navigate a new path.

Let's stop just surviving this motherhood journey and start thriving. I am here to walk alongside you as you move toward becoming the mom you truly want to be.

Shall we begin?

xx

Dr Hilary Claire

CHAPTER 1

RELEASE

WHAT'S HOLDING YOU BACK AND HOW TO BREAK FREE

Women can do anything, and we are, but we are now doing everything (or close to it).

I lost myself in motherhood

I went into motherhood knowing that I wanted to be a playful, attentive, energetic mom *and* keep pieces of myself as an individual. I wanted to continue to create meaningful work as a clinical psychologist helping other women live their best lives and helping children to be as healthy and happy as they can be. I wanted to be kind to mother earth and be part of the solution to help restore her so my kids could enjoy the wonder that she had to offer.

Somewhere between the sleepless nights and endless diaper changes, however, I lost my compass. I went into survival mode and all those glittering ideals of what I thought my motherhood experience would be got murky. I remember days where it was just about getting to the next nap time. I found myself praying for Luke to get home early from work. It took all my energy to do something simple, like choose what to make for dinner.

Why was it so hard? How had I arrived in this place? I had been a very capable, optimistic and energetic person pre-baby, but that seemed like a bit of a fantasy now.

I remember many afternoons walking the beach while Oak napped pressed against my chest in the baby carrier and won-dering what had happened. I didn't know who I was anymore at all. I didn't know what I was feeling. I had no idea what I even needed. I had been so caught up in caring for Oak and just getting through each day that I had lost who I was, who I wanted to be and what I wanted my life to be about all at once. Even more discouraging, it felt impossible to get back.

Mamas, before we get into all the details, I'm here to tell you that *you* are still within you, even during this time. I know this because some part of my academic mind was still within me during this haze. I became curious about why I was depleted, experiencing burnout and just surviving day to day, especially when I thought I had been prepared for it. I also started ques-tioning why this was so common for mothers in general.

I felt so alone in this struggle, but as I talked to other moms, read postnatal research and sought expert knowledge, I realized I was far from alone. It wasn't just me! In fact, it seemed to be most mothers. And while I learned that it may be *common* for mothers to struggle with this exhaustion, loss of control in their lives and loneliness, I adamantly refused to call it "normal" – that's society's word and I believe we can do better for mothers. Through my research, clinical work and personal lived experience, I have come to know that we can.

What to expect in this chapter

In this chapter, we will look at the leading reasons why modern day moms are operating from a place of fatigue and overwhelm as their norm. These are some of the main causes that stood out most prominently for me personally, in my research and in my clients' experiences. We'll unpack common societal expectations, nutritional health influences, unhealthy stereotypes and isolation.

With the knowledge that we are not alone in this struggle and an understanding of why this is common, we can empower ourselves to take back our power, to move out of burn out and start thriving in motherhood. As you read through, consider what causes are most relevant for you.

THE LEADING CAUSES OF BURNOUT IN MODERN MOTHERHOOD

So, what gets us into this situation of overwhelm and exhaustion anyway?

The reasons go beyond the physical toll that carrying, birthing and breastfeeding takes, which in and of itself is no small feat. It also goes beyond the wake ups we have for weeks, months or years depending on our child's sleep patterns – no doubt these also contribute.

What a lot of us don't realize until we're deep into overwhelm is that there are physical health and nutritional reasons, practical realities and societal norms that layer on mothers making it harder for us to stay vital as we navigate motherhood. It is unconscious most of the time, but these subtle messages shape us and how we approach our motherhood experience. Let's explore!

PHYSICAL HEALTH AND NUTRITIONAL MATTERS

Postnatal depletion is real

A major reason why modern day mamas are struggling begins with their physical health; their bodies are significantly depleted and inflamed. Pregnancy, birth, breastfeeding, and all the strains that come along with motherhood nowadays can lead to a deterioration both physically and mentally. This is postnatal depletion; a syndrome that is an accumulation of issues such as intense fatigue, overwhelm and even hyper-vigilance. Add broken sleep and reduced sleep quality and quantity that is common when you have a baby and this burnout can be significantly amplified.

Postnatal depletion is often insidious. It slowly creeps into new mothers' lives. For many, it isn't until years down the track that the symptoms really add up. Dr. Oscar Serrallach, the doctor to have coined the term postnatal depletion, states that on a societal level, things have to change to more fully support mothers. But he also emphasizes that many moms are literally depleted of essential nutrients to keep them healthy, well and vital.[1] And nutrient depletion can be a pretty major health issue that can manifest all sorts of challenging symptoms.

Zinc, iron, magnesium, vitamin D, B vitamins, iodine, selenium, vitamins A, E and K2, and omega 3 fatty acids are just some of the micronutrients that mothers are often depleted in. Many of these are associated with the fogginess, fatigue and poor concentration that are all too common for mothers.[1,2]

How exactly do mamas become lacking in these critical nutrients you may ask? There are all sorts of reasons:

- the food we eat
- medical conditions
- some medications
- exposure to toxins
- our modern-day lifestyles
- pregnancy
- birth
- breastfeeding
- subsequent pregnancies

What a lot of women don't realize is that they often go into pregnancy already depleted of adequate stores of essential vitamins and minerals. Why? Because eating nutritionally well is something most of us struggle with. Combine that with the loss of micronutrients that results from the growing, birthing, caring for and feeding our babies and you have a compounded condition impacting mothers on your hands.

Unless these micronutrients are replaced, the depletion and subsequent health effects get worse. If you took a good quality prenatal vitamin then you are off to a better start. However, these often don't have adequate amounts of key nutrients for the individual mama due to some of the reasons we will go into now. And many moms stop taking these after birth.

The plight of fast food

There are some very real lifestyle factors that lead to further nutritional depletion for moms; what we eat is one of them. At the best of times, it is challenging to eat a super nourishing diet. We live in an age of convenience. Throw a fussy baby who refuses to sleep into the mix and all of a sudden, the temptation to reach for pre-packaged food becomes even more irresistible. While packaged and fast foods may be an easy solution at our fingertips to keep the 'hangry' away, they typically don't offer any high nutritional value. The priority of these items is on food storage rather than nutritional density.

The standard western diet puts our bodies under stress and doesn't give us adequate nutrients. We can easily get enough calories but we cannot get enough nutrients if we eat this way. Our bodies are not designed to handle the amount of sugar, vegetable oils, processed foods or artificial additives that modern day foods commonly contain. It is hard for our bodies to process and use. For instance, excessive sugar can strip our bodies of essential nutrients and energy.[3,4] So too can food additives like synthetic preservatives, colours and flavours [5,6]

Even if you eat impeccably, there may still be nutrients that you are low in because of the deficient mineral content of much of the soil it is grown in. Industrial agriculture is stripping the soil of critical nutrients and healthy microbes. If it isn't in the soil, the plants we eat will struggle to have these nutrients in them. Also, suppose you are eating dairy or meat products from factory farms. In that case, those animals, unfortunately, will likely not have excellent nutrient content simply because of the poor quality feed they are given.[1,7,8]

Damaged microbiomes impact our health

Some conditions like autoimmune diseases, intestinal absorption issues and low stomach acid can make it harder for you to replenish your micronutrient stores.[1] For instance, there is the issue of damaged microbiomes that is all too common nowadays. The gut microbiome is made up of bacteria, yeast and other microorganisms that if in a healthy balance, keep us healthy too. Unfortunately, in our modern world, there are many things that can damage the delicate gut microbiome. Some main causes are antibiotics (those used personally and ingested through factory farmed dairy and meat products), certain medications, chronic stress, poor sleep, the typical westernized diet and not eating enough fiber. Even your own birth (cesarian sections particularly lead to a less ideal microbiome) can impact your microbiome. Damage to the gut microbiome can hinder the process of food digestion and nutrient absorption. So even if you are eating an amazing diet, you might not be benefiting from all that yummy goodness.

You may not be absorbing all of the nutrients from your food because of a myriad of other reasons including not chewing enough, low stomach acid (if you have heartburn or indigestion - it usually isn't from high stomach acid as many believe but low stomach acid) or eating in a rushed or stressed state.[9]

Medications and our body's nutrients

Naturopathic doctor, Dr. Jolene Brighten, emphasizes in her book, *Beyond the Pill*, that the oral contraceptive birth control pill can leave the body lacking in many nutrients including zinc, selenium and B vitamins. She emphasizes that these nutrients are also the ones that help the body create calming neurotransmitters, balance hormones, regulate our immune system, and keep the thyroid happy among other critical processes.[10,11] The last thing a tired mama needs is less calm-inducing neurotransmitters or out of whack hormones, am I right?

The pill can disrupt the gut's microbiome making it harder for the body to properly absorb the nutrients that it does ingest. With so many women ceasing their use of the pill only shortly before trying for a baby, this is not an issue to be overlooked. Further to that, moms often go back on the pill between pregnancies – often at the six-week postpartum mark. This is a time when moms need as much nourishing goodness as they can – not to be robbed of any further nutrients!

Exposure to environmental toxins

Similar to how the strain of artificial additives in foods drain the body of nutrients, so too can other toxins from our environment. We are all exposed to a huge number of environmental toxins in our everyday lives. These include air pollution, car exhaust, mould, ingredients in cosmetics, shampoo, cleaning products, and even perfume. Chemicals even leach into our food when we heat it in a plastic container in the microwave or from the lining of many disposable take out coffee cups. It takes energy and nutrients to process and excrete these from the body – not to mention the health risk associated with these chemicals.

Our modern lifestyle

Our modern lifestyles can also be tied to our inadequate nutrient levels. For instance, insufficient sun exposure can lead to very low levels of vitamin D. Now, I am not advocating for sunbathing or burning, but a little bit of sunshine on our skin is something that our bodies require. How often do we go from our homes to our cars to our workplaces and back again and never get any sunshine or fresh air? Our bodies' processes weren't designed for these indoor living arrangements and need some outdoor time and even a little bit of sunshine on our skin.[12]

Then add pregnancy into the equation...

Then pregnancy comes along and further depletes our depletion. As does subsequent pregnancies, breastfeeding, stress and sleep disruption that comes with the younger child-rearing years.

Pregnancy takes a toll on our bodies. Babies get the best nutrients first while growing inside of us and so they should. But we, the mothers, are then left with whatever is leftover unfortunately. Depending on our lifestyle and diets, that might not be enough. Thanks evolution!

Even morning sickness (which I experienced as 'all day sickness') can limit what you are able to stomach and therefore reduce your ability to eat an adequate amount of certain foods or even tolerate a multivitamin.

Subsequent pregnancies in quick succession can further strip away our nutrient stores. The body may not have had time to fully recover and build up adequate stores of essential nutrients before giving so much to the next growing baby. In our society many are having babies later and living very busy lives, so nutritionally replenishing our bodies after birth is often the furthest thing from our minds. Losing the baby weight and getting your pre-baby body back gets plenty of play time in our society. Holistically building up your body's pre-baby nutrient stores? Not so much. Especially if we want to have more children, optimizing these nutrients between pregnancy is crucial not only for our babies' optimal development, but for ourselves too!

Something that my husband's most significant mentor in his medical training said has stuck with me. He said that there is all of this emphasis on eating more in pregnancy, but it is during breastfeeding that you need to up your calorie consumption. I couldn't agree more. For those of you who currently are or have breastfed, don't you remember your ravenous appetite and voracious thirst in those early months? I certainly can! My thirst is still triggered the instant I start feeding. My point is that babies get amazing nutrients from breast milk, but that also means that mom is being stripped of those amazing nutrients herself if she isn't maintaining an impeccable diet and likely supplementing certain nutrients.

I breastfed Oak until he was 21-months-old and I was 2.5 months pregnant with his little brother. As I write this book, I am currently still going with Moss who is 19-months-old.

While I enjoy breastfeeding and am an advocate for all of its amazing benefits, I know it takes a lot from the mother. Fast forward a few years when baby is getting into solid foods and mothers still often face nutrient depletion challenges. We are so busy making the best organic, veggie-packed meals for our kids that we forget to sit down and eat a good nourishing meal ourselves. And that habit becomes a way of life that steers us further away from life as a vibrant mama.

PRACTICAL AND PERSONAL REALITIES

Modern living is taking a toll on our health

Another marker of a modern mama burnout? The norm of the busyness as the norm. Chronic stress, which has also been tied to a drop in nutrient levels. Chronic stress uses up a lot of our stores of important micronutrients like magnesium, zinc, iron and other nutrients. It also takes a lot of energy. So, if you are living a high paced, chronically stressed lifestyle, you may be putting additional pressure on your body's nutrient stores.[13,14,15,16,17,18]

Unmet expectations of birth and early parenting

It is challenging to adjust to the realities of parenting and the stark contrast between what you expected motherhood to be like and what it is. Those of us who have perfectionistic tendencies (hand up over here) can struggle greatly with this transition, the lack of consistency and control and the unknown. Our expectations are often vastly different from our current realities and sometimes, we are pushing ourselves to attain something impossible. Life is messy with little ones. It is nonlinear. 99% of the time, it isn't glamourous like it appears in many Instagram feeds. And just when you think you have something figured out, your little grows and everything changes once again.

Our motherhood journeys often look drastically different to what we planned for right from the beginning. Some mothers go through unexpected conception struggles. Others find themselves nauseous and puffy during pregnancy instead of glowing like they had wanted to. And many more mothers have births that look nothing like what they wrote down on their birth plans. Then when our little ones are earthside, we quickly discover that they have minds of their own. We can't simply follow the instructions in a manual and *get it right*, and the amount of control we have over any given situation has greatly lessened. For instance, you may think your baby should sleep all night or you have been told that she should sleep a specific number of hours every day, but she may have other plans.

While going for what we want is amazing, holding on too tightly to our expectations – particularly about ourselves – can hold us back from embracing motherhood as it is and keep us stuck frustrated, exhausted and disappointed.

Moms take on much of the new parenting responsibilities alone

And now for the really "fun" part of all this – in western culture, moms take on much of the new baby responsibilities alone. Being a mom is a hell of a lot of work. So, the question needs to be asked, "How can she possibly take care of a brand-new baby and herself at the same time?" With many moms now without the traditional village or family living nearby, much of the baby burden is on them alone. The practical barriers of not having grandparents, aunts and uncles or siblings to call on and share the responsibility of child rearing creates a massive strain on the parents. Often the partner has to work to support the growing family and the mom is left alone with a baby.

There are no breaks, no downtime or me time from the constant demands of children. Paid lunch breaks no longer exist. Peeing alone suddenly feels like a luxury (friendly reminder: it is not). Moms are becoming more isolated, more disconnected and spending a great deal of time at home alone with their little ones hidden away from the rest of society. And they're suffering as a result.

Carrying for our little ones is a 24/7 job that falls predominantly on the mother nowadays. Throw in a traumatic birth, many of us having babies later into our thirties and forties, and little down time to recover due to the demands of our busy lives, and you have a recipe for exhaustion right from the get-go.

Forget about mom, there's a baby here!

When you are pregnant, our western culture treats you like this beacon of light. Everyone is so excited and happy for you. You are showered in attention, gifts and help. Then the baby comes and that all ends. From that day on it is all about the baby. People ask:

"How is the baby sleeping?"

"How much does he weigh?"

"Is she teething?"

"Is she eating well?"

Even the medical system lets women down. Once you have the baby there is no focus on your health and wellness as a mother anymore and it is all about the baby from now on – other than the quick six-week check that pretty well just has the doctor telling you to go on birth control.

Naturally there is going to be a shift in focus and that is fine. But new moms can get lost in this and feel selfish or like a bad mom if they take time for themselves and basic selfcare. This is a breeding ground for shame, guilt, and negative beliefs about what a good mom is in a time when new moms are quite vulnerable. Recently there is more awareness about the importance of mom's recovery from birth and the birthing of a mother that happens alongside the birth of the baby, but in mainstream society, this doesn't get much airtime.

SOCIETAL EXPECTATIONS

Your beliefs and expectations may not be your own

Our beliefs are shaped by those around us, the media and the society we grow up in. Most of these beliefs are unconscious and developed at a very early age. The way our parents divided household tasks, the way moms were portrayed in books and movies, and the subtle ways that mothering is viewed by society all make their way into our personal philosophies through which we make sense of the world. And the unbelievable part is that this happens without us even being aware of it or actively doing anything. Some of these beliefs are helpful, but some that we take on don't serve us well. We often unconsciously reinforce these beliefs as we grow older and become moms ourselves.

Old societal norms that may have worked when women were not allowed to have careers are continued to be passed down, often without intention or awareness (like most norms and beliefs are). Not only are these wildly outdated, but they are often very unhelpful and hindering. While few people may be directly stating these expectations, they are still hanging on in our culture and show up in indirect, subtle ways. For instance, one common expectation is that moms do the lion's share of the child-rearing and take on most of the household tasks, such as family organizing and cooking. This no longer fits with the world we live in where mama also has a full-time career to manage – and yet these outdated norms pervade. I will note that societal norms are always in flux and do not pertain to all people in a society. For some families, mom is not the one who juggles the majority of the mental load and that is fabulous!

What you believe, you unconsciously bring into your life and create your reality around. So, choose the beliefs, societal norms and expectations that you want to guide your life – otherwise you will likely end up living according to the mainstream con-structs. And these might not be doing you any favours. Not sure what I mean? Let's take a look at two prominent norms: the selfless mother and the supermom.

The societal norm of the "selfless mother"

You can probably already picture the "tired, selfless mom" before I describe her, because this stereotyped role is baked deeply into our society. She is expected to put everyone else's needs before her own, even if she is tired and in desperate need for some support herself. It is considered perfectly normal to be tired – after all, society will say, that's motherhood for you!

Typically, in the western world, it is moms who carry the bulk of the childcare workload. There is an underlying expectation to look after the kids, keep track of the family's scheduling, get everyone to and from their appointments at the right time and play nice within family politics (if there are any). And she is expected to do so selflessly with a smile at all times. Who cares what she needs though, she's a mom now, right? Now her role is to just support everyone else and make sure they flourish.

"PS: Don't forget to keep the house sparkling and that birthday party organized with a homemade birthday cake that looks like a perfect replica of the team from Paw Patrol. We know you're tired, but you're a mom now – that's just how it is," love society.

And as a member of that society, we often blindly buy into this expectation. Many of us have unintentionally taken on these beliefs.

There are plenty of messages in society that subtly or not so subtly suggest that exhaustion, depletion and loss of self are just part of motherhood. Do any of these sound familiar?

"You'll get time again to create that business you want when the kids are older."

"Being tired comes with the terrain of motherhood. I haven't had a good sleep since my first was born."

"My iron is low and my hormones are all out of whack but that's what happens when we have babies."

I get it. It is hard to balance desires and realities for most, if not all, of us moms. But chatter and small talk like the above is reinforcing that it is just normal for moms to feel this way and that we have no power to change it. We just have to power through.

We can change it, however, and the first step, I would argue, is changing the language we use to speak to exhaustion in motherhood – it is a *common* condition, but it shouldn't be regarded as *normal*, nor should it be expected of us to endure in silence.

Stop calling us "supermoms"
Once the expectation of being a "tired, selfless mom" is absorbed, we're often then led into a second destructive stereotype – this expectation of being supermoms. A "supermom" is expected to be happy all the time as they do everything for everyone else. In fact, the people around them regularly exclaim, "I don't know how you do it all!" because the scope of what she is taking on for everybody else requires a massive output of energy. And while the term "supermom" may seem flattering at first, maintaining this role inevitably leads to disappointment, exhaustion and discontent in motherhood. It is an impossible expectation that cannot be achieved or maintained.

Modern day moms are often in the middle of a rising career when they begin having children. This pressure to hold everything together, including being the primary carer 24/7, maintaining the household, their career, and nurture their relationships has mothers overextended, rushing and exhausted. It is a far cry from the motherhood bliss that many of us dream of, that's for sure.

Many moms are stretched thin across their many roles, as they try to do what they could do before having kids while also being a full-time parent. It is unsustainable and exhausting but only part of the problem. We're not superheros, we're mothers who need and deserve support to thrive.

The feminist movement has made so much progress for women's rights. As women, we're now able to go after our dreams and have careers outside the home that not many generations ago were completely out of the question. I am forever indebted to the heroic women's suffrage movement who made my path through life filled with so much more freedom, choice and ease. We are told we can do anything that a man can and every day women are proving this. Getting an education, becoming a professional, mastering a craft, climbing huge mountains, becoming prime minister (in some countries anyway) are all possible and even normal now for women. Great news for us all!

But some things have yet to catch up. Women can do *anything*, and we are, but we are now also expected to do *everything* (or close to it) in many ways. This is most evident when we become mothers. Women have not only taken on roles that were stereotypically that of a man's, but we have kept the typically female roles too. The result? A double workload that often goes unnoticed.

Particularly as mothers, but it often starts before that, women are taking on the 'invisible load' – the invisible, emotional, practical load of keeping everyone and everything sorted in the household or family on top of having great careers, relationships and community involvement. Mothers get stuck in "doing it all" and we're tricked into thinking "doing it all" is a good thing by being called "supermoms" by society. We're tricked into thinking that being able to do it all at the expense of our own wellbeing is a sign of strength.

However, supermoms don't exist, and the term is not a flattering one. None of us can do everything well, all the time and be able to enjoy our lives in the process. Yet we see this mom ideal of doing everything herself everywhere. We internalize it and then try to attain it. Mothers are bombarded, consciously or not, by unhelpful pressures and outdated ideas of 'selfless mothers' and 'supermoms' from all angles. Social media, other mothers in mothers' groups and even mothers from older generations all perpetuate these unhelpful stereotypes that we absorb and believe as a life truth.

How many Instagram accounts can you think of where moms show their perfectly curated homes, impeccably dressed kids, and something delicious that even Martha Stewart would envy sizzling in the kitchen for dinner all while rocking a career? I can think of a few. This version of motherhood is promoted by mainstream media everywhere – magazines, shows, movies, even product commercials – and we subconsciously buy into its message of "do it all" and "do it all by yourself."

This version of motherhood has become the aspirational norm.

As we become moms, we unconsciously try to stretch ourselves to fit this version of motherhood no matter how uncomfortable or exhausting it might be – and by doing so we indirectly pressure other moms to do the same. What silliness!

Incredible past generations fought for our freedom of choice. Now it is our turn to fight for the next generation of girls to not have to do it all, but to do what feels right to them on their own terms. We can't take on the roles of men, keep the roles of women, add mothering to it all and keep it up. Something has got to give.

The first thing to go is the belief that a woman who asks for help or says no to taking it all on is weak or unsuccessful. We have to pick what our priorities are, work with our partners or hire external help to support us with these tasks. Keep in mind, those shiny Instagram accounts from before that we all follow rarely post about the nanny or housekeeper who is working in the background to keep everything picture perfect. You can ask for help too!

Most importantly of all, we need to start being proud of the choices we make and what we do, and lose the false sense of pride that lingers around being and doing everything all the time.

Why do these stereotypes exist?

Even with all of the progress that the feminist movement has made over the generations, our society is still heavily patriarchal. This masculine dominance informs the decisions about maternity leave (and paternity leave), childcare subsidies and other policy decisions that predominantly affect mothers. This creates systemic barriers that make mothering an upward battle for all modern day mamas from day one.

Some workplaces are slowly shifting away from the typical, yet highly outdated and ineffective (in most fields) 9-5 work schedule. There is a slow transition to more flexible hours, part-time work, extended maternity leave, and having child-friendly workspaces, but this progressive change is in its infancy. The majority of workplaces are governed by rigid work rules and strict 40-hour work weeks and often, due to financial pressures, mothers have to choose whether they go back to their careers fully or not at all.

While positive shifts are happening all the time, we live in a society that I would argue doesn't adequately value the role of mothers. Messages from our society even devalue mothers sometimes. The perception is often that stay-at-home moms don't do *real* work. "*What does she do all day?*" is the common question from the outside looking in. After having kids, I quickly realized that going to a "job" is much easier than parenting day in and day out.

Parenting is damn meaningful. What can be more important than growing, raising and shaping the future generation?

Crunching numbers, going to meetings or writing books, no I don't think so. In no way is my intention to downplay the conventional jobs that we get paid for. All of these contribute to our society and the future in their own ways, big and small. But I want to emphasize the significance of mothering and how this has, and continues to be, undervalued in our patriarchal society.

Mothers are paying the price for how our society currently operates. There is a noticeable lack of support enabling her to navigate the balance (for lack of a better word) between being a mother and maintaining her career. But we can be part of the shift even when there are systemic barriers like those mentioned above working against us. True change starts with each one of us!

WHY NOT BEING EXHAUSTED MATTERS

Now that we've explored some of the physical and societal reasons for exhaustion that are all too common for mothers nowadays, I hope you can make better sense of your unique circumstances and have a greater understanding of why you are having a hard time in motherhood. It's not you, it's the world around you, the society you live in and the effect both have on your perceptions and belief system.

While the reasons we've explored are very real and extremely challenging, with the awareness of them and committed action to change your path moving forward as a mother, you can rise above all of these. You have the power to find your way out of burnout, to take full responsibility for yourself, your health and your thriving as you move forward. In doing so, not only will you be empowered, but your kids will benefit from having an incredibly strong woman raising them and you will shift the journey of other mothers around you and to come after you.

As you go through your day and week, start noticing what subtle and insidious influences are keeping you from being a vibrant mama. With awareness, as modern day moms, we have the power to let these go and rise above.

When you rise, you take others with you whether directly, by modelling a different way or changing ingrained, systemic norms for the better.

You can be vibrant. You can do the great things you want to do and you can be the most incredible mama while enjoying the process for yourself.

YOUR NEXT STEPS

It can be helpful to understand how you got where you are before moving on to creating the future you desire. Here are some questions to ask yourself to get more clarity on some factors that have led you to exhaustion, overwhelm or disconnection in motherhood. Take a couple of minutes to think through these, grab your notebook and see what comes out.

- Which of the reasons discussed in this chapter seem highly relevant in leading you to be a burnt out mama for you personally?
- What are some other societal, situational, beliefs, lifestyle or personal reasons you have found yourself just surviving motherhood?

- What is it specifically about your lifestyle that is keeping you stuck in exhaustion?
- Does the food that you eat help or hinder you?
- What societal norms or beliefs do you have that are holding you back from thriving in motherhood?
- Are you trying to live up to the supermom stereotype or accepting that as a mother, exhaustion is just par for the course?

THINGS TO REMEMBER

Physical health and nutrition matters

There are a number of physical and nutrient reasons why moms are struggling. This includes:

- Modern day food lacking in nutrients
- Many of us having gut and absorbency issues
- Certain medications we take can deplete our nutrient stores
- Pregnancy, birth and breastfeeding take a lot from our bodies
- Broken sleep

Practical realities

- Busy lifestyles are taking a toll on our health
- Expectations of how our lives will be when become mothers often don't align with our actual reality of motherhood
- Moms don't have adequate support and take on much of the parenting alone
- When a baby is born, all of the attention and care is given to the baby but no one is mothering the mother
- Moms take on the lion's share of the invisible load

Societal expectations

Many societal expectations make it challenging for modern day moms to thrive during motherhood, including:

- Unhelpful beliefs about what a 'good mom' should do pervade our society
- The stereotype of the tired, 'selfless mother' is all too common
- The other mom stereotype is that of the 'supermom', which is impossible to live up to

Why not being exhausted matters

- You can rise above these reasons keeping moms stuck.
- You can thrive.
- By being empowered and taking responsibility for your life, you are modelling this selfcare and empowerment to your little ones and other moms.
- You are creating societal shifts in each step you take.

CHAPTER 2

IMAGINE

HOW TO ACTIVATE YOUR DREAMS INTO REALITY

*When you are thriving, there is suddenly so much more
love, joy and ease in motherhood, relationships and life
overall. Clarity is the essential first step toward this.*

Realizing motherhood could be more

During that first year of being a new mom, any opportunity
I had to get together with other moms, I was there. I craved
social interaction and especially wanted to be around others
who were also newly navigating this motherhood journey. (Side
note: Years later, some of these amazing women have become
my closest friends.)

At one particular park get together with a few of these mom
friends, our fleet of baby carriers and strollers sprawled on the
grass, we got on to the topic of how tired, stressed and irritable we were. Several were talking about how life wasn't what
they expected it to be as a mother. The general theme of that

afternoon? That the unrelenting nature of being a full-time caregiver was wearing us down.

As we sat on our picnic blankets watching our little ones toddle about and climb around the play structure, we laughed about how trying and tiring it can be to just get organized and out of the house on time in the morning – let alone consider having time in the day to rest. One of my good friends, Lily, remarked that perhaps during the first few years of our kids' lives, just surviving is probably good enough.

"Maybe we can thrive again in a few years," she sighed. "But this isn't our time."

While my intention certainly isn't to put pressure on anyone to live up to unattainable expectations, I believe I would be doing other moms (and myself) a disservice to accept that exhaustion, depletion, loneliness, irritability and overwhelm should simply be our lot for several years (read that again, *years*) because we chose to be mothers. There has to be another way, another option to operate from without adding to our stress. I also don't see that being struggling mothers who just get through the days is going to be of great benefit to our children. We deserve more and so do they.

There is no question that during the early years – and likely forever – our lives will look much different to how they did before kids. That's is okay – even great in many ways. I am not here to say that we should strive to have that pre-kids life back while mothering too. I personally don't want that. My values, interests and priorities have shifted significantly and there are aspects of my former life and identity that I am not interested in resurrecting. However, moms should be able to be in a space where they enjoy their lives, can prioritize their health, do meaningful work and still be great mothers.

After Lily raised this issue of simply surviving, I challenged my friends with some opposing questions. "What would life be like if you *could* be vibrant *and* a mom? If exhaustion, guilt, irritability or feeling inadequate were no longer issues for you, what would you be doing? How would you be acting? What would you focus your time and energy on?"

Well, the floodgates opened. Their faces seemed to brighten, and their eyes glimmered wistfully.

"I would do more yoga."

"I would feel excited about being a mom."

"I would get back into running again."

"I would get my hair cut more often and maybe style it once in a while."

"I would sleep better."

"I would finally start that business I've been dreaming about."

"I would go on dates with my husband again – and we would talk about at least one thing other than diapers and poop."

"I would be more patient with my kids."

"I would be more fun with my kids."

"I would hire a cleaner."

"Every little thing wouldn't seem so big and insurmountable."

"I would read a book with no pictures or cartoons in it."

"I would feel less tired."

"I would go swimming in the ocean more often."

"I wouldn't feel like I was doing it all on my own."

"I wouldn't be feeling so lonely."

"My baby would sleep!"

"I would get up early in the morning and have five minutes to myself before the kids woke up."

"I don't even know what I would do. I don't even know where I would start."

I was amazed by all the ambitions and dreams that bubbled forth. It was as if nobody had asked this question of them since the two lines appeared on the pregnancy test. It was incredible to watch these thoughts resurfacing as possibilities.

For most of us, that day was a wakeup call that we were not living in alignment with what mattered most to us. Sure, we loved our kids immensely and wanted the best for them, but the rest was a bit out of whack. Most of us were spending a huge chunk of our days cleaning, chauffeuring, organizing life admin tasks, getting snacks sorted, doing the shopping and maintaining the household. While many of these things have to be done, we were spending a disproportionate amount on them. Between taking care of the kids and household stuff, there was little or no time for anything else in our lives. We were exhausted as we went about these tasks and certainly not prioritizing our own needs or wellbeing as we went.

And, as I discovered through my research, the truly sad thing of it all is that we weren't the only ones living this way.

Many moms are cramming their professional work into the fleeting minutes and hours when kids are napping or once they have finally fallen asleep. For those that do their work outside the home, they are racing from the moment they get up in the morning to the time they crash into bed at night, trying to get everything on the to do list done – feeling guilty as they go. You know the to do list I'm talking about it; meet all of the kids' needs, build careers, maintain the family's commitments and household, socialize, workout, meal plan, meal prep, then cook... it goes on and on.

And as if that wasn't enough already, for most of us, we are trying to do it all by ourselves. We are burning ourselves out in the process of trying to be everything to everyone. It was scary to realize that our lives resembled those of 1950's housewife with a twist of doing it all a bit more than we would have liked to even admit to each other. And in the process, we were losing our spark and ourselves.

This conversation got me thinking about how it can be possible for modern day mothers to thrive. How can we be vibrant mamas? We can bring these aspirations into being if we first know what a vibrant life looks like to us personally.

Once we are clear on what we want, our minds can open up to find ways to make this dream a reality and we can actively build this into being. With awareness, direction and consistency we can move toward being vibrant moms and leave depletion, exhaustion and discontent behind. And opening up our minds to the possibilities and dreams that we have for our lives is where we are starting.

What to expect in this chapter

In this chapter, you will get clear on what you want for your life broadly and on a day-to-day basis. Getting clear on what you want helps to inform the choices you make going forward, what you make space for in your life, what you fill your time with and where you devote your energy.

The purpose here is to open you up to what you want your life to be about and teach you how you to best support yourself so that you can flourish not only as a mom, but in all areas of your life. You will begin thinking about your values, priorities, decisions and where you focus your attention, time and energy.

I would highly recommend that you have a pen and notebook nearby so you can write down some reflections, ideas and actions as you go through the chapter. After all, as we all know, life's busyness has a habit of getting in the way and can make us forget about the specifics of an idea if we aren't careful. There are several questions throughout this chapter, which when answered honestly will help you to solidify what you want more easily. If you are more of a speaker than a writer, feel free to do voice recordings of the activities in this book. Do what feels best for you.

As you go through this chapter, be gentle with yourself. It is okay if you are not where you want to be exactly right now. That's why you have this book in your hands, to learn, to grow and to empower yourself with change. Be as detailed as possible about how you want to show up and what you want your life to be about. Allow yourself to sit in abundance without constraints of reality for the moment. You can go back to the massive laundry pile and demands of your current day very soon. Just give yourself this time first.

A little mind trick

During the activities in this book and especially in this chapter, focus your attention on what you want rather than what you don't want. Our minds are terrible at distinguishing between *do* or *don't*. They just focus on what is.

For instance, if you focus on not wanting to feel anxious and tell yourself, 'Don't feel anxious. I want to stop feeling anxious. I never want to feel anxious again!" your mind focuses on anxiety. And what it focuses on grows.

Instead, focus on what you *do* want. If you focus on thoughts like: "I want more calm in my life. I want to relax more. I want to breathe deeply and find more ease in my life," then your mind will start noticing those little moments of calm and spaciousness already present in your life. Your mind will also start coming up with ways to bring more relaxation into your life.

This is a much more helpful place to work from, so keep it in mind.

YOUR VIBRANT LIFE

Cast your mind forward into the life you want – whether that is one year or five years from now. It is up to you. Paint a picture of what's to come in detail. Imagine that you are living a life that supports you in feeling happy, energized and confident. You may not be feeling this way right now. You may be feeling exhausted or stressed. But give yourself some space to imagine the future that you want. There are no right or wrong answers here. It is about finding what works best for you.

Your mind might be screaming at you right now saying things like, *"This is ridiculous. I am never going to feel energetic or calm! What's the point in imagining this?!"* Thank your mind for trying to protect you (our human brains find any change, even positive change scary). Then see if you can set these thoughts aside for a few minutes.

It is important that you first clarify what it is that you want to make your life about and be specific. Really specific. Otherwise, you can spend your life drifting and quickly end up getting lost in the exhaustion and overwhelm of tending to everybody else's needs. Defining what matters most to you and creating a structure based on this is a great way to stay on track. But before we get to the specifics, let's take a little time to dream. You may even find it a little bit of fun!

How to get started

You can simply read through this section and visualize your answers as you go, or you may want to read through and then sit quietly with your eyes closed to imagine your ideal life for a few minutes. I would suggest the combination would be most effective at getting you crystal clear on what you want and what matters most to you.

Put your little one down for a nap or find a time when they play by themselves for ten minutes. Ideally have your partner take the kiddo out to the park for a bit so you can enjoy this activity without having to listen for any cries or calls. Grab a cup of tea. Curl up on your favourite chair or go sit outside in the sun. You may even like to put on some calming music. Then take a moment to dream.

Phase one:
Preliminary questions to reconnect with yourself
Reconnect with what energizes you. Consider what brings you vitality. Project yourself into the future and see the vibrant you. This version of you is calm, confident and content in motherhood and in your life overall. Now answer honestly:

- What does your ideal future life look like?
- What are you doing in it?
- How do you feel?
- What do you focus your time and energy on?
- Who do you spend your time with?

Now let's get a little more specific. Continue to visualize how your future vibrant self would act and live, but in more detail.

Phase two:
How do you wish to be seen
Picture how you spend the majority of your time and energy.

Notice who is there with you. In this phase you're going to focus on the aspects of life that are going to be of the highest importance to you.

- ◆ Visualize your relationships with your partner and kids. Notice how you act toward them and what activities you do together.
- ◆ Envision your work outside of family life. If a career specifically isn't something you are interested in having in your future, replace 'work' or 'career' with volunteering, hobbies, studies or any additional tasks you want to be involved in. How are you spending your time in this aspect of your life?
- ◆ Imagine what your partner, kids and friends say about you. What characteristics and qualities would they use to describe you?

Phase three:

Nourishing yourself

The vibrant you takes impeccable care of herself. You now prioritize healthy habits because they enable you to keep doing what it is you love doing. Pay attention to what you are doing to support your health. Visualize yourself taking care of yourself. This might be going for walks in nature, dancing with your partner in the kitchen, getting to bed before nine, or sourcing healthy premade meals from a local café. Answer honestly:

- ◆ What foods are in your kitchen? What meals are you eating to nourish your body?
- ◆ How are you keeping your body strong?
- ◆ What are you doing to relax?

- How are you bringing more joy into your life?
- How are you ensuring you are getting the support you need?

Phase four:
Ditching draining habits

You no longer struggle with perfectionism, comparison or hold onto old, unhelpful identities. You can manage your time and energy without running yourself down. That means that you have stopped wasting your time doing unnecessary things. You have also delegated necessary yet draining tasks to someone better suited for them, because vibrant mamas say yes to support and ask for what they need.

- What parts of your former life do you no longer wish to carry with you?
- What specifically has the vibrant you let go of?
- What limiting beliefs, societal expectations, cultural norms or old habits have you left in the past?
- What are the draining habits that you no longer waste your finite resources on?
- What supports or systems do you have in place to help you balance motherhood and your other priorities?

Take your time

This is a great exercise to come back to over and over. This may sound a bit *woo woo*, but stick with me. The more you envision who you are being, what you are doing and how you are feeling as a vibrant mama, the more you will step into being this. You will begin making decisions from this perspective. You will begin acting aligned with this version of you.

My personal vision

For me, I envisioned a life where I felt calm, abundant and connected. I was spending my time cooking beautiful, healthy dishes for my family, not because I had to, but because cooking was a joy. I was writing books, creating courses and running retreats to help mothers thrive while also helping their kids to be as healthy and happy as can be. I was spending plenty of time with friends and family and set up a small work team of supportive, passionate and caring women. I was taking walks in nature, doing yoga and living a walkable lifestyle. I was being silly, patient and cuddly with my kids.

My family and friends were describing me as being kind, healthy, grateful and accepting. My kids said that I was playful, caring and present. I was getting plenty of support in all areas of my life so I had time for what mattered most to me – my family, friends, health, nature and creating meaningful work. There was a simplicity and ease to my days, weeks and years with plenty of gentle but consistent routines and rhythms to make it flow easily. For instance, I had a short and simple morning ritual to set myself up well for the day to come.

But that's for me. What does a thriving life look like for you? Is it similar? Is it wildly different? Visualize your ideal. And write it down so you don't forget.

YOUR THRIVING DAY

Continue to project yourself into this desired future life. Now let's narrow it down to your daily life. Let's get even more detailed. Answer the following questions as if you are this future vibrant you.

What does your ideal day look like – one in which you are thriving?

Imagine your ideal day. Notice what it is that you are spending your time and energy on.

- What are your top priorities?
- Consider what habits you engage in daily to keep you healthy and bursting with energy.
- Who is there with you?
- Define what supports you have in place to help you thrive in your many roles each day.
- Consider how you feel, what you are thinking and what you are paying attention to.

What do you do in the morning to set you up for an energized day?

Watch yourself move through your morning. Notice where you are and who is with you as you move through your morning.

- What time is it when you wake? Is this before or after your little ones have woken up?
- What do you do first upon waking? Then what? Move through your morning routine noting what habits you do to set you up for a great day.
- What do you eat and drink? Do those things bring you joy?

- What rituals do you do to prepare yourself to have more calm in the day to come?
- How do you integrate taking care of yourself while helping your little ones start their days off well?

How do you set yourself up in the evening for calm, connection and rest?

Now make your way into your evening. How are you spending your evening? Who is there?

- Begin moving through your evening. Pay attention to the routine you have in your evening to close your day calmly and prepare yourself for rest.
- When do you eat dinner?
- Who do you spend your evenings with?
- How do you help your little ones get prepared for rest?
- What routines and rituals do you including in your evening to prepare yourself for rest?
- What time do you go to sleep?

Getting clearer

Now that you are getting clearer on what it is that sets you up for a great day and a vital life, you can start making choices and taking action aligned with these. When making decisions see if you can make them from the perspective of this future thriving you instead of from the stuck place you may find yourself in currently.

Consider what the future vibrant you needs, how she acts, what support she seeks out and how she would set herself up to enjoy her life. As you progress through this book, you will delve deeper into how to do this and start taking intentional action. The clearer you are initially, the smoother the journey will be.

THINGS THAT ARE KEEPING YOU STUCK

If you're honest with yourself, you're likely doing things at the moment that are keeping you stuck. First things first, that's ok.

I have had plenty of moments of staying stuck and still find myself there from time to time. The good news is that it does get easier to move out of burnout when you have clarity about where you want to go and consistently take little steps to get there. So, to make these little steps easier, let's identify what exactly is keeping you stuck.

Here are some of the barriers myself, my friends and my clients talk about when it comes to feeling stuck:

- Staying up too late.
- Not being clear on what we need.
- Quickly eating on the run.
- Comparing ourselves to other moms.
- Spending too much time alone at home with our little ones.
- Saying yes to everyone else's requests, even when we don't want to.
- Not asking for support.
- Staying indoors on our phones scrolling social media.
- Holding onto societal stereotype like 'Moms are just supposed to be exhausted.'

What are some of the things that you are currently doing that are holding you back from living the life you desire?

What beliefs, choices, actions and habits are keeping you stuck in survival mode?

The "stuck" me vs the vibrant me

When I am not being my version of a vibrant mama, my morning ritual is being woken up by kids crawling on me and demanding my attention immediately (we co-sleep and when they are awake, they are literally in my face). When I am stuck in overwhelm, my morning looks like me trying to brush my teeth, make lunches and get kids dressed while they are needing cuddles, needing to be picked up and wanting to be played with. I can easily feel very rushed, stressed and guilty. On these days I feel my energy leave me and a surge of cortisol (aka the stress hormone) takes over. I am left exhausted before 8AM. Not ideal.

But this chapter isn't about that stuck version of you or me. It is about the one that takes care of herself, is intentional with her choices, life and how she spends her time.

The vibrant me knows that she needs time, care and organization before she can be a caring and attentive mom. She recognizes her own needs, like having a few minutes to herself before the rush of the day hits. She talks to her husband about how important these seemingly little things are for her mood and energy and how much nicer her company will be for the rest of the day if she can attend to these little things for herself.

So, the vibrant me sneaks out of bed after Moss has drifted

off again after his very early morning feed. She quietly goes downstairs and makes a cup of loose-leaf green tea. She takes it outside and sits for a few minutes. She does some slow deep breathing or a ten-minute guided meditation. Then Oak comes downstairs and they make breakfast, cookies or go for a short walk to the beach together. She has already packed lunches last night and organized her work bag the evening before. Instead of feeling exhausted like her counterpart, she feels invigorated, connected and calm by 8AM. She has already made her day successful on her own terms. And she has made space for joy.

And on those nights when she was woken several times by children? She allows herself to get a few more minutes of rest in the morning. When the kids wake her upon waking themselves, she lies there for a minute, takes a couple deep breaths and reminds herself of how she wants to show up that day. It isn't as energizing, but being flexible and kind to herself when things don't go exactly to plan (because as we all know, kiddos are often on their own time) is just as important.

So ask yourself – does your morning set you up well for your day ahead?

LOOKING FORWARD

So, you know what you would like and have some ideas about what is keeping you from getting there. Now what? Let's compare where you are headed now versus where you want to be headed.

First picture your life as it is right now. Consider how your life will be one year from now if you continue doing what you are doing. If you keep making the same decisions, letting the same beliefs guide you, and engaging in the same habits that you currently are, consider where this might lead you in one year.

Then project yourself five years down the track. Imagine what your life will look like then if you continue spending your time and energy how you currently do. If you were to keep doing what you are doing, what would be the worst thing that might happen? What might be the best thing?

Now, let's do the same thing but imagine that you have started making changes to create a life that supports you fully to be vital, joyful and at ease. Imagine how your life might be one year from now if today you start letting go of unhelpful expectations, created a support network, and allowed new helpful habits into your life. Think about the impact that these shifts would have on you, your family, your careers and all of the other aspects of your life. Now go even further to five years from now. Consider what amazing things might come from your efforts.

I know it might seem all too hard to picture how you are going to get from where you are to where you want to go but stick with me and we can do it together with many small steps. And getting crystal clear on what you want and what's holding you back is the really big first step. You did it!

HER STORY:

MARISSA, MOTHER OF 3

Marissa, 31, has a two-year-old daughter, a four-year-old son, and is pregnant with her third child. She loves being creative with her kids and going on all sorts of nature adventures with them. She also enjoys writing about her parenting philosophy and wants to support other parents who share her values. But there never seems to be enough time in the day for what she loves.

HER "STUCK" FEELING

She currently works full time in a position that pays well and offers job security, but the work is dull, and she finds being stuck inside all day draining. She rushes home after work, juggles dinner and bath time and does her best to squeeze in some playtime with her kids. After she's put them to bed, she finds herself dropping in front of the TV and binge-watching Netflix. More often than not, she falls asleep on the sofa and wakes up around 2AM to go to bed properly. In general, she feels exhausted, uninspired and overwhelmed.

HER VISION

When she focused on and wrote down her ideal day, she saw herself spending more quality time with her kids and working a job that she loved. Marissa saw her days looking slower and calmer with her priorities being family, work that lights her up and spending more time in nature.

She realized that the way she currently spends her weekends is how she wanted her future weekdays to look – creating fun activities for the kids, going to the beach, hiking with friends, and sharing meals with extended family.

Through this exercise, Marissa realized that she wasn't going to find fulfilment in her career or more time with her growing family if she didn't make some changes.

HER ACTION

Marissa felt a bit overwhelmed at the thought of making several changes to how she spent her time, but was also excited to think about the possibilities for her future. Marissa started thinking from a place of her future vibrant self and as a result, her actions mirrored her intention. She began by focusing on getting better sleep and spending more time outside on her lunch breaks. She also committed to spending more time outside when she was with her kids. These three small actions were manageable in her current lifestyle and started to move her in the direction she wanted her life to go.

HER NOW

When I met with Marissa several months after the birth of her third child, she was continuing to prioritize an earlier bedtime and was outdoors for a couple hours every day. She would let her baby nap outside in the shade as she played with her older kids. She was also setting up a parenting coaching business with the aim of getting this underway before her maternity leave was up at the end of the year. This would enable her to work from home and be more available to her kids, which aligned with the ideal day she envisioned for herself. Through small, consistent steps governed by clarity, she was embodying her vibrant future self more and more as time went on.

What would the vibrant you do?

A handy question to always have in the back of your mind when making decisions or when someone asks something of you, is "What would the vibrant me do?" This simple question will enable you to choose and act from your future perspective rather than your current stressed-out state. This is so helpful because the mindset that got you to where you are now likely won't get you to where you want to go. A new upgraded perspective is needed.

You may want to come back to this chapter in future and spend a few minutes imagining exactly what you want your life to be about. Doing so can help you get clear and focused on what matters most to you. The more you get clear on what you want, your subconscious mind starts believing it could happen and therefore can help your mind to find ways to bring your reality closer to this vision. Now, let's start to get our spark back!

YOUR NEXT STEPS

Over to you now! If you haven't already, write down in detail what you imagined during the visualization exercises outlined earlier in this chapter. Answering those questions will help you gain clarity on your true desires for your life on a day-to-day basis.

Give yourself the gift of ten or fifteen minutes (or longer if you can!) for some reflection by answering the following questions.

Your vibrant life

- What would your future life look like for you to be vibrant?
- If you were no longer just surviving motherhood but thriving, what would you be doing?
- What would you be spending your time and energy on?

Your thriving day

- What are you currently doing in your day that you would like to carry forward into your vibrant future?
- What does your future ideal day look like?
- How does your future vibrant you set up her morning for a successful day?
- How does the future you set up her evening for calm, connection and contentment?

Things keeping you stuck

- What are some of the things that you are currently doing that are holding you back from living the life you desire?
- What are the beliefs that aren't your own that are holding you back?

Looking forward

How would your life be one year from now if you continue doing what you are doing? If you keep making the same decisions, letting the same beliefs guide you, and engaging in the same habits that you currently are, where will this lead you in one year?

How would things be one year from now if today you started making decisions guided by your future vibrant self? If you start letting go of unhelpful expectations, create a support network, and allow new helpful habits into your life, where might you be in one year?

THINGS TO REMEMBER

A little mind trick
- Make change easier on yourself. Focus your attention on what you want in your daily life more than what you don't want. Your brain has a hard time differentiating between do and don't.

Your vibrant life
- Clarity about what you want your life to look like is a critical first step in creating it.
- Get crystal clear on the future vibrant you: how she treats herself and how she spends her time.

Your thriving day
- The vibrant you is intentional with how she spends her days and who she spends it with.
- She creates a simple, doable morning routine that sets herself up well for the rest of her day.
- She also is purposeful with what she does in her evenings to help herself wind down from the day and sleep well.

Things keeping you stuck
- We all have beliefs, choices and habits that do not set us up for success in our days.
- Becoming aware of these allows you the opportunity to alter them.

Looking forward

- If you keep doing what you are doing, you will likely stay stuck.
- If you make positive shifts in your habits and routines, you may find yourself in a very different place – a place with daily practices and people around you to support you to be the best version of yourself.

CHAPTER 3

PRIORITIZE

DISCOVER THE ONLY TO-DO LIST THAT
REALLY MATTERS IN YOUR LIFE

*Prioritizing your health and happiness is the greatest
gift you can give your children.*

Positioning priorities

During the first year of being a mom, I was with my son pretty
well all day, every day except when I would teach the odd yoga
class or take a shower. But if I am being honest, he was usually
right there in the shower or crying to get in. It was all too easy
to put my son first all – the – time.

Luke was busy in the last year of his medical training and wrote
his final exam a week after Oak turned one. So as much as he
was caring and supportive, he had commitments that kept him
away a lot. His evenings were either spent at the hospital or
studying. I didn't acknowledge how much more I needed from
him until I was already burnt out. And time together just the

two of us? Forget about it! In that first year, I could count the number of times we didn't have our little man right there with us on one hand. In all the busyness and exhaustion, we certainly didn't prioritize our relationship.

I exclusively breastfeed so I was the one up in the night to feed him. Oak hated the stroller but napped really well when he was in the baby carrier, so I carried him around strapped to my chest for hours every day. If I did put him down for a nap in bed it was a struggle to sneak away without his little sleepy hand grabbing me. Isn't it wild how aware babies are even when they are asleep?

We lived across the world from our families in a new town where we didn't know many people. And as a new mom, there was no way I was going to trust some random babysitter with my tiny baby. So, the care of our little guy was on me. In other words, he was the number one priority and that started to wear me down hardcore without me even realizing it at the time. I didn't give time to myself, my relationship or the things that kept me happy, healthy and fulfilled.

My priorities were all out of whack. Baby, baby, baby and whatever else baby needs.

Naturally, our babies are going to get lots of our attention and care, and they absolutely should. But I let myself and my relationship slide *way* down my priority list and many much less important things took up residence near the top of my list without me being aware. What kind of less important things? Well! My preoccupation with always having a clean house for starters, moving house more often than I'd like to admit, travelling overseas several times, overly accommodating others and trying to make all my own personal care and baby products from scratch (because that's what the perfect eco mama does, right?).

Oak went everywhere with me, including my sessions with my psychologist (yes, psychologists go to psychologists). During one particular session, I was standing, gently rocking him to sleep in the baby carrier when my psychologist said something I will never forget. "You need to be your first priority. Your partnership needs to be your second. And your child is your third."

And she claimed that that was what was best for my son! I was shocked and thought she was out of her mind. I mean, that was not the behaviour I had seen modelled anywhere in real life, in the novels I read, in the movies I watched or in the social media I consumed at the time. What was she talking about? And even if she was right, that just seemed too hard to actually do.

Honestly, it took many years, until I was a mom of two, for her message to finally sink in. As a psychologist and recovering perfectionist, this is a hard thing for me to admit. She was absolutely right, and I wish I had taken that message on board when I first heard it. I might not have gotten to the point of such depletion if I had. But now, years down the road, here I am writing the book about exactly this – and you might be rolling your eyes as I once did!

So let me say it one more time – mamas, you need to be your first priority.

Why taking care of yourself first is essential

Taking care of yourself is the best way you can take care of your kids. Our kids need us to be our personal best so we can be the best mothers to them. If we are stressed, exhausted and fighting with our spouses all the time, how can we possibly give our kids the attention and love they deserve? We can't. They need us to be healthy, happy and supported so we can help them to be the same.

When I look back now at my first few years of being a mom, I genuinely wonder how I got through it all. I wasn't anywhere on my own priority list. I was suffering. My health was declining. My marriage was shaky. I was running on empty. And despite desperately pushing to put my little ones first, it wasn't even beneficial to them because they weren't getting the calm, happy and attentive mom *they* deserved. I was impatient, foggy, and drained. Sound familiar?

Are you also putting too many people and commitments above you on your priority list? The answer is probably yes, otherwise you wouldn't be reading this book. If you are, first of all be gentle with yourself. After all, you're likely facing some or all of what I faced – nutritional deficiencies, societal stereotypes and cultural expectations. And guess what? You are not alone in this struggle. This is all too common for moms. We get suckered into the idea of putting everything and everyone else first by powerful external forces. And the worst part is those external forces that expect this mindset from mothers revere this approach to motherhood. How ridiculous is that?

It's a vicious cycle. It's hard to break free from. But it's not impossible. Cycles can be changed, and you can live your motherhood journey differently.

What to expect in this chapter

It is all well and good to picture a future where you are vibrant and being the mom you truly want to be for your little ones, like we did in the previous chapter. But this next step is a critical piece in moving you toward that vision.

In this chapter you are going to get crystal clear on what you must prioritize to create a future where you can move from exhaustion to being energized, so you can do the things that matter most. It all comes down to what you prioritize. And you, my friend, must become your number one priority. Your relationship with your partner is second. And your children are third.

It's okay to be shocked. It's okay to think I'm completely wrong. It's okay to roll your eyes. Remember, I did all of those things when my psychologist first presented me with this concept.

But I'm here to tell you from my personal experience and extensive research that this is the formula. It is that simple (not necessarily easy though). Now let's get into the details.

PRIORITIZING YOURSELF: WHAT DOES THIS EVEN MEAN?

I once saw a friend post on Facebook thanking his wife for how selfless she is and how she always puts her family and community first. And what ensued in the comments? All sorts of congratulations.

"I don't know how she does it all!"

"She is totally an inspiration!"

"I wish I could do half of what she does!"

Such sentiments might be well meaning, but sadly reinforce the negative "supermom" stereotype. Moms are expected to be selfless, to be able to do it all on their own and to not go completely bonkers? Uh!

Being selfless is NOT a good thing. It is in fact damaging. I hate that the term 'selfless' is so casually used as a positive way to describe 'good' mothers. Being selfless burns through emotional, mental and physical resources. Being selfless leads to exhaustion, moodiness and resentment. Being selfless destroys the individual, the mother, who is at the heart of the family unit. It is unsustainable.

I'm reminded of what flight attendants tell us time and time again: "It is imperative to put your oxygen mask on before helping others." Why? Because if you're passed out on the plane you won't be any help to anyone. It's a similar premise with motherhood. The only difference is that nobody questions the flight attendant.

Moms are no good to anyone else if we are overextended, drained and going a bit batty. That's certainly not the recipe for being the kind, present and fun mum I want to be. How about you? Taking care of yourself does not make you a bad mom. It means that you care so much about your kids and your family that you want to be the best version of yourself for them.

Just as my wise psychologist told me, as a mom you have to be clear on what is important to you. The first priority is yourself, second is your relationship with your partner and the third is being a parent. (Yes, I realize I've said this before now, but it is worth repeating to allow it to sink in.)

This certainly does not condone neglect, but it does emphasize the importance of taking care of yourself so that you can be a better caregiver and happier human in the long run. Healthy and happy parents who have a solid, supportive relationship with one another are much more able to show up for their children as the best parents they can be.

Why prioritizing yourself matters

If you get anything out of this chapter (or this book for that matter), let it be the message that putting yourself at the top of your priorities list is one of the best things you can do for yourself, your family and society. Big call, I know. If moms take care of themselves, they show up as the best version of themselves, and this has noticeable ripple effects on their kids, the positive contribution they have on others and the world. And don't forget about the positive impact you can create if you have your energy and spark back.

I struggled to wrap my head around the counter-intuitive concept – that looking after myself first wasn't selfish, but actually kinder for my entire family. When you look after your own needs first, you are more energized to hold space for others, whereas when you are depleted, overwhelmed and chronically stressed, you have less capacity to help, serve and support others.

If we don't take care of ourselves, we often don't act in ways that we would be proud of, nor do we give our best to our endeavours or to the people we connect with. When we are stressed or exhausted, we go into survival mode which makes us closed off and have less capacity to be generous or kind. Why? Because we simply do not have the energy. You wouldn't expect a car with no gas to keep running, would you? Eventually it will breakdown and everybody will say, "Oh of course! It needs more fuel!" Mothers are similar – we need fuel to be energized.

A depleted mom might snap at her little ones. She may put them in front of the tv instead of playing with them because she is too tired. She may reach for the frozen pizza instead of a nutritious home cooked meal. She is doing her best, of course, but her best on limited self-resources likely isn't the vibrant mama she dreams of being.

When I see to my needs first, I find that showing others kindness, appreciation and generosity comes with ease. And this attracts more kindness and love back to me. It is an amazing feedback loop!

Imagine if your default was to prioritize yourself first? Think about it for a moment. If you were well-nourished, exercised, showered and fulfilled by interests beyond your home life, how would you feel? How would that feeling translate to your mothering? What would your home life look like then?

Prioritizing yourself is a gift to your children

We all want the best for our children, right? The best food. The best schools. The best holidays. The best extra-curriculars. And we'll move mountains to get them the best. So, let me ask you, is giving them the best version of yourself on that list of must-haves? If not, why? Don't your kids deserve the best mama too?

Think of a time when you were exhausted. Were you the mom you want to be in this moment? How did you respond to your kids' tantrums or needs at this time? Were you patient and kind or grumpy and snippy? I certainly didn't show up as my best self when I was burnout! Nope. I snapped more easily, felt flustered and even had a little tantrum of my own sometimes. Unfortunately, this usually left both me and my child even more upset and exhausted.

Now consider a time when you were well rested, when you had spent time outside, enjoyed nourishing foods and even taken some time to see friends. You were feeling content and healthy, right? How did you treat your kids then? In these times, I show up with more patience and take the time to understand what unmet needs might be lurking under my little one's meltdowns. I am able to be the calm, stable adult for my boys to feel safe and heard by. Their challenging behaviour usually passes a lot more quickly when I have the strength and energy reserves within me to show up like this too.

Notice the difference in your parenting during these two moments. If you are like the majority of us, you too found it a whole lot easier to parent the way you want to when you were feeling good.

Prioritizing yourself teaches your kids by example

Our kids are constantly watching us. They watch how we take care of ourselves, how we talk about ourselves, how we nourish our bodies, what values our lives are guided by, how we treat our partners, how we interact with friends, and how we deal with challenges. This list goes on and on.

They make sense of the world by watching us. The values they live by begin with us. How do you want your little ones to treat themselves and others? What sort of role model do you want to be for them? Deciding to prioritize yourself is the first step.

When you love yourself, it shows. It isn't about being overly confident or conceited. It is simply about caring for yourself like you would any other important person in your life. This models selfcare and self-respect for our kids. We cannot expect them to feel secure and strong in themselves when they are out in the world facing challenges if we don't act this way first. You want your kids to grow up to be independent and capable adults who care for themselves. The greatest way to teach this to them is to model the behaviour yourself. By taking care of ourselves, they learn this is a normal and healthy thing to do throughout their childhood. They will take that into adulthood too.

Be the example for your kids. Better yet, live the example for your kids.

How to prioritize yourself when it goes against everything you've been taught

You might ask, how can I possibly be my first priority? I certainly did. I had no idea where to begin.

In your busy life you must consciously take time for yourself. One way to prioritize yourself is to make time for the things that make you feel nourished, joyful and relaxed without letting feelings of guilt get in the way. Guilt will hold you back from following through on your own selfcare and it has no place in the life of a vibrant, joyful mama. So, say it with me one more (yes one more) time – put yourself at the top of your priorities list.

Prioritizing yourself can also look like:

- Going to sleep when your baby does in the evening.
- Turning off social media notifications on your phone.
- Saying no to requests that are not an immediate "hell yeah."
- Seeking out like-minded mama friends.
- Letting go of sky-high expectations of yourself.
- Hiring a cleaner.
- Eating nourishing meals full of organic, unprocessed goodness.
- Dropping the beliefs that you should or can be supermom.
- Getting outside daily for a bit of sunshine and movement.
- Dividing household tasks between you and your partner.
- Making decisions from the perspective of your future vibrant self.

My on-going journey

Years on, I am still working my way out of the unnecessary burnout I caused myself by refusing to see myself as a top priority. But it gets so much easier. The biggest step was shifting my mindset and asking myself two questions:

"What would the vibrant me do?"

"How can I prioritize myself today?"

There were other big changes like getting some help with the house cleaning and finding a family day care that I felt comfortable sending my boys to. But it was in the little micro steps and daily habits that I created by asking those two questions over and over again that really got my journey out of postnatal depletion moving. It was taking a couple slow deep breaths when I started to feel overwhelmed. It was getting out for walks when I was feeling isolated. It was paying attention to my emotions and being curious about the unmet needs behind them. Those were the things that moved the needle for me.

Did I always remember to prioritize myself? Absolutely not. It took time to build this muscle and it is still something that I grapple with today. But I am getting better at remembering to do so, finding ways to prioritize myself and following through with it. I see the benefits it brings now and that is my motivation to keep it up.

I am a much more present and playful mom because I prioritize myself and my wellness. I not only gift myself time to do the things I enjoy, but I ensure I take regular breaks from parenting. Sometimes these breaks are five minutes, six hours and even a couple times overnight.

What will you do to prioritize yourself more? I'll give you a hint: reading this book is a great start. Implementing what you read here is even better. And simply the mindset of prioritizing yourself is often all it takes to start creating real change.

HER STORY:

REBEKAH, NEW MAMA

When Rebekah, a friend of mine, was pregnant everyone gave her attention - her partner, friends, colleagues, and even strangers were overly accommodating, caring and excited for her. People asked how she felt, told her that she was glowing, and gave up their seats for her. She had so much attention from health professionals too with all of her doctor appointments, blood tests and ultrasounds. Everyone was excited for her. So was she and she grew accustomed to this extra attention as her belly grew.

Then one day it all stopped. It was the day she gave birth.

HER STRUGGLE

Her attention was immediately on her new little one, Noah, and so was everyone else's. The questions became all about the baby.

"Was he a good sleeper?"

"Is he eating well?"

"Was he hungry?"

"Was he growing well?"

There were regular doctor appointments to weigh, measure

and check baby milestones. There were gifts of baby clothes, rattles and swaddles.

For Rebekah, like many mothers, she had her six-week check up with her doctor and was then left to her own devices. As the weeks progressed, no one asked how she was faring, if she was resting enough or scrutinizing her food choices anymore. She was essentially left alone with a brand-new baby and a brand-new life landscape to navigate.

Sound familiar?

Without realizing it, she too put all her focus on her beautiful new baby. Everything she did revolved around when he fed, slept and pooped. He was priority number one and really the only priority for months. But Rebekah started crumbling. She wasn't sleeping enough and was eating on the run. In the busyness of new motherhood, she hadn't allowed herself the time and nourishment to heal her body after the pregnancy and birth. And it was all starting to take its toll.

HER REALIZATION

I recall Rebekah telling me, "I can't think of the last time I actually sat down to eat a meal with Andy (her husband) or even when the last time we chatted about something other than Noah."

She bashfully mentioned that she snapped at Andy often. Rebekah realized something was wrong when she found herself losing her patience with her baby. She was not feeling her best and was deeply frustrated with how her usual carefree nature had been replaced with stress and anger. Something had to change.

HER ACTION

Rebekah began considering what she needed and asking for support. Specifically, she started taking small breaks from mothering to go for walks, eating meals slowly and showering without a squishy baby in the bathroom with her. Once she realized that taking care of herself was critical it was easier to make decisions that supported her to thrive and focus more on her own health without guilt.

HER NOW

Within a few months she noticed her stress levels lowering and found a greater patience for the little things that used to send her off the handle. Rebekah continues to check in daily with herself to see how she can support her highest self and plans to continue doing this until it becomes second nature. She is even taking herself to Pilates classes twice a week and having conversations with her hubby about topics other than babies!

Prioritize yourself by taking care of your little ones

Taking care of your kids can also be a way of putting yourself first. Consider it a little life hack for mamas. Caring for yourself doesn't have to be completely separate or mutually exclusive from caring for your kids. I don't want to add more to your already overflowing plate. Let's make it easier on ourselves, okay?

For instance, I don't give my kids candy, sweet drinks or

processed food that contains any artificial ingredients. While it is much better for their health, mood and development, it is also great for me. I choose to feed them only healthy food, so I don't have to deal with the peaks of hyperactivity and the crash into tantrums that so often follows consuming processed foods (it isn't just my observation, these things are backed by research)[19-24]

During my post graduate training with the Australasian College of Nutritional and Environmental Medicine (ACNEM), paediatric doctor, Dr. Leila Masson drove this point home. She emphasized that food additives along with several other aspects of our diet and lifestyle can have a huge impact on our kids' brains. Food additives are often a contributing reason that kids appear to have more severe issues and even get labelled with mental health disorders. (Just to be clear, I am not saying ALL mental health issues for our kids come from their food and lifestyle, but there is more and more evidence for the significant impact food choices have on our kids and on us. It is something to be aware of).[24,25]

These food-like substances can really mess with the brain and mood, causing normal, healthy kids to act like they have an attention and hyperactivity disorder. I have experienced this myself and you may have too. For me, dealing with the extreme mood, excitement and come down cries drain my energy like nothing else.

In my life, I go on and on about the studies I read regarding how our food impacts our mood, stress, and brain health – especially those that are about the effects of these things on children. Poor Luke has to hear about them all of the time. I am passionate about feeding our kids the freshest, organic wholefoods without any strange sounding ingredients. In the beginning of my food fascination, Luke went along with it but thought I was maybe being a bit extreme. He wasn't sure it was really that bad if the kids had some junk food until one time when Oak was 20 months old and we hired a new babysitter.

She was warm, kind and highly recommended. She sent me photos of Oak over the afternoon. He was happy playing in puddles, colouring and eating. But I saw he wasn't eating what I had left with him. He was eating a cupcake with colourful icing and a big red lollipop! This was nowhere near the organic, homemade food I was obsessed with feeding him and had left with instructions.

Oak was like a different person when we came home. His mood was all over the place and so was he. He was teary to the point of being inconsolable. He screamed at anything we said to him. It was almost like he wasn't himself anymore which was distressing for all of us. That evening was exhausting. It took all of our attention and energy to soothe him, hold him as he cried and allow him to act a bit wild as the chemicals and sugars worked their way through his little body.

Once he finally settled that evening and he drifted off to sleep, we relaxed, thinking the worst was over. But that night he had night terrors. It's the only time my baby boy has ever had night terrors. Being woken up by your kid shrieking is terrifying and heartbreaking. After this experience, Luke was very onboard with not giving him any more processed food for quite some time. The cause and effect in our child was undeniable.

My point is that by prioritizing good food for my kids, I am prioritizing myself too. By serving wholesome food to my kids, I end up eating healthier too without it being an 'extra thing to do.' I also don't have to deal with the wild moods and melt-downs. And I don't have to deal with the begging and tantrums when I don't give them these sugary foods. My kids don't really know what mainstream processed foods are, so they are happy enough to eat real food and are convinced that dates and almond butter are the best treats ever.

While this does get harder as they get older, I'm enjoying the ease it brings to my home during this phase of life. I am the one who chooses what food arrives on their plates and they choose how much to eat; I choose to prioritize my health and wellbeing and therefore theirs too.

Other ways to prioritize yourself by taking care of your little ones

So ask yourself, how can you prioritize yourself while taking care of your kids at the same time? Is there a way of parenting, sleeping or eating that makes it easier on both of you?

Maybe it is playing with your little one outside, racing around after them, picking them up and rolling around on the grass. This play time together will not only help fill up their cup with quality time with mom, but it can also be a great way for you to get some fresh air and a workout.

As your kids get older, you can teach them to take slow deep belly breaths when you notice their emotions starting to heighten. In time this will give them an incredible skill to help regulate their emotions and you will have a calmer kid because of it. Even in the teachable moment, practicing those belly breaths will help you slow down and relax too.

Getting your kiddos into a relaxing evening routine can be of great benefit to you both as well. It will help them begin settling down by knowing what happens next and thus giving them a sense of control. This routine can help your nervous system to calm down too and prepare for a more restful sleep.

Do you see how modelling the healthy habit empowers your kid and your role as a mother?

Prioritizing yourself is as simple as making intentional choices. Is this choice moving me toward the vibrant mama I want to be or further away from this reality? Get used to asking this question around everything you do, and you will start taking much better care of yourself in the process.

PRIORITIZING YOUR PARTNERSHIP

Parenting, partnerships and prioritizing – this could be an entire book on its own! When my marriage is strong, when I feel supported and when Luke and I are acting as a team, motherhood isn't half as challenging as it is when we are disconnected, playing the blame game or seeing each other as adversaries. There is an ease and reassurance in having each other's back. We are both better parents for it. But we have also gone through times when our relationship wasn't so strong, and I know my kids didn't get the best of either of us during those shaky patches.

I can recall one day in particular when I got angry at our new toaster not working very well. Luke said that I was being too negative and that this wasn't good for our kids to witness. While he may have had a somewhat valid point (don't tell him that), I did not receive it well in the moment. At all.

What should have been received as a constructive comment felt like a personal attack. And I responded as such. Couldn't he see I was doing *everything*, and this toaster was the last straw? The answer is of course not, because I wasn't communicating clearly how I was feeling lately or how hard everything was becoming for me.

He saw his wife in the morning, went to work, and then saw his wife in the evening, who said her day was fine. He didn't see the challenges of an entire day at home with just the kids for company, because he couldn't be there and I didn't share the hardships. The result? A morning of feeling 'fine' dissolved into moodiness when I was trying to do something as simple as make toast. Oak didn't get to play hide-and-seek with me, and Moss didn't get cuddles, because mom and dad were having a standoff.

What I realize now, is that our communication as a couple had changed, but we weren't aware of it at the time.

Like me, you may have trouble trying to be a present, calm and attuned mother if you are resentful, angry, hurt, or arguing with your partner. You cannot give what you want to your kids when you are caught up in relationship struggles. Even if you don't think your relationship issues are affecting your kids, my guess is that they are. As we know, kiddos notice everything. They notice that you are not able to give them the attention they crave because your mind is preoccupied. They read your emotions through your body language even if you try to hide it. They can sense when mom and dad aren't happy.

The reality is that parenting is a tough gig and your relationship can easily take a backseat as a result. It is all too easy to get stuck in a cycle of blame, anger and resentment when you are deep in sleepless nights and endless diaper changes. No question that having kids changes a marriage and can easily strain it. However, if you prioritize your relationship, it can become stronger and you can both feel more supported than ever before. And everyone, especially your little ones benefit from that.

Keep in mind also that your kids witness how you deal with relationship challenges. You are their model for future relationships. You want to show what a healthy relationship looks like to your kids, so they learn and go on to have great friendships and relationships throughout their lives. When you do the work to prioritize and strengthen your relationship, your kids get happier parents who are more capable of giving them quality time. They also learn how to show affection, kindness and deal with conflicts in healthy ways.

{NOTE: I recognize that families are all different. Some moms have partners, some co-parent, some have their kids half the time, some raise their kids alone and others rear their kids in more of a village set up with a few key carers around. Some kids have two moms, some have two dads, some have one mom and one dad, while some have one main parent. These concepts can be applied to any relationships with the key person or people in your life with who you are romantically involved and/or play a major role in the raising of your kids. I will be using heteronormative terms, but please insert whatever designation is most appropriate for you.}

Practice clear communication with each other

How many times do you say something to your partner, only to have them interpret it in a completely different way which then causes confusion or conflict? And vice versa? That's okay! Clear communication skills take practice.

Even though I work with clients to improve their communication, it is a skill I too aim to improve and is front of mind on most days. I may know how to say something in a more helpful way but that doesn't mean that I always choose to do so. Psychologists can be petty and stubborn too in their personal lives unfortunately (we're all only human) but with awareness we too can improve.

Here are a few fundamental communication tips to help you start connecting clearly with your partner and reducing defensiveness.

Communication Tip 1:

Nobody is a mind reader

First, remember that your partner cannot read your mind and know what you want, need or are thinking. If only it was that easy! I am always shocked at how differently Luke and I interpret situations and communications. Too often we think we are on the same page about something and then later realize we were so far off base. Now we try to be crystal clear about everything from how we are feeling to who is putting the sunscreen on the kids before daycare. When we assume things, we often get it wrong. Remember to express yourself out loud.

Communication Tip 2:

Words matter

Second, instead of saying "You are *always* late to get home and I have to do *everything*!' consider dropping these extreme words. Those words are antagonising. Does your partner always do something or just often? Test out replacing "*always*" with "often" and "everything" with "a lot." The words we use may seem insignificant, but they can have a massive impact, both positively and negatively.

Another great little shift of wording is instead of saying "You are... (being mean, selfish, lazy, unhelpful or not caring about me...), add "My mind is telling me the story that" to the beginning of your sentence.

So, the communication changes from, "You don't care about me and what I need," to "My mind is telling me the story that you don't care about me and what I need." Notice the difference?

The second approach takes some of the heat out of what you

are saying. It creates some space and lessens the sense of being attacked. This way, your partner will likely feel less defensive and thus be able to hear what you are saying without anger, guilt or fear clouding his mind. (None of us humans can think very well when we are feeling intense emotions. It pretty well shuts down our prefrontal cortex which gives us the capacity to think rationally, make good decisions and take on other's perspectives).

Communication Tip 3:
Consider the motivation
Third, when the urge to blame, criticize or attack enters your mind, consider what is most important to you: do you want to 'win' and be right or do you want to have a healthy, happy relationship? There certainly are ways to get your opinions across but pushing to prove you are right and that your partner is wrong or at fault rarely gets you what you want in the long run. It doesn't even get them to do what you want in the first place!

A final fundamental communication tip
Finally, simply saying sorry goes a long way. None of us are perfect. We all make mistakes but owning and acknowledging them is a pretty powerful thing to do. In fact, it is very strong and courageous.

So ask yourself – how can you communicate more clearly and kindly with your partner today?

Be gentle with yourself and your partner
One of my favourite things to remind myself of is that everyone, including my husband and I, is doing the best that we can with

what we have, what we know and how much energy we have. We are all trying our best, even though we all get it wrong sometimes. Let's just try to be accepting and kind to ourselves and others, why don't we?

A relationship exercise: Enjoy each other's company

Jump forward into your future together. Imagine a snapshot of you and your partner in five or ten years.

- How are you acting toward your partner?
- How are you feeling toward him?
- What would you like to say to him?
- What activities would you be doing together?
- How are you acting as a team and supporting your partner?
- How are you communicating your needs, emotions and challenges to him?

If you are having difficulty coming up with answers, think back to before you had kids or when you started dating. Take your mind to a happy moment you shared. Spend a couple of minutes remembering this time. Notice what you were doing and how you acted toward each other. What aspects of this relationship do you want to take with you? What do you want to create more of?

Prioritizing time together outside of parenting can keep your bond strong and help you to see each other as more than just co-parents.

How to begin

I would suggest journaling about what comes to mind. Be as specific as you can with how you would like to treat, talk to and feel toward your partner and what activities you would do together. The natural tendency is to focus on how you would like to be treated and talked to but focus on what you can control which are your actions and words – not your partner's.

Brainstorm some ideas of how you could move in this direction within your relationship. Would that be telling your partner exactly what you visualized or how you want to stop blaming and instead be kinder to each other?

At the moment it may feel like too much to work on prioritizing your relationship, but the work it takes now will pay off in dividends. When you let go of blame, communicate clearly and kindly, enjoy time together and show up as a united team, you will be making huge progress toward that vibrant life you want. Plus, you're essentially bringing in loving, capable and effective support for your day-to-day life, so you don't have to do it all.

Build a support team

A final piece to further prioritize your partnership is to create a greater support team. First, consider how you and your partner can be more of a team and support for one another. But recognize that you cannot be everything for each other. It is an unrealistic and unhelpful expectation that so many of us have nowadays since we are living more and more in pods of two disconnected from the greater community or living far from family.

I cannot be Luke's support for everything nor can he be mine.

When I forget that, I inevitably become disappointed, but I am also reminded that I need to seek out friends, mentors, professionals and other moms for the support that Luke cannot give me. For instance, I do not go to Luke for support and guidance with writing this book. He has never written a book, nor does he want to. He encourages me with the book and offers emotional support, but I instead turn to my editor and book coach for more specific support. I do go to him when I need to vent about the challenges of my day with the kids, but I also might take this to my mom friends who are in the thick of this daily as well.

When considering your own partnership, ask yourself:

- Who are other key support figures in your life right now that you can turn to for advice, validation and a listening ear?
- What practical supports can you seek out for maintaining the household chores and invisible load of motherhood?
- Who could you call or visit if you are feeling lonely?
- Which health professionals can you meet with to support you with improving your health, increasing your energy and boosting your mood?

PRIORITIZE YOUR BIG VISION

It's time to start putting some pieces together. Think back to the Vibrant Life you imagined in the previous chapter – the future that supports you being the vibrant mama of your dreams.

Let's start to identify the elements in your life that are essential to you.

Here's the exercise: imagine that all responsibilities and expectations have disappeared. Essentially, you have a blank slate. You are free to dedicate your time and energy to whatever your heart desires and you can spend your time with whoever you choose. Create three to five categories of focus; areas of your life that you envision your future vibrant self happily spending time on.

For me my areas are:
+ my relationship with my family and friends
+ my health
+ my career helping create healthier mamas, kids and communities
+ my connection with and protection of the natural world

For you it may be spirituality, your family and your community. And for someone else, it might be their marriage, saving dogs in developing nations or furthering their own education.

The following are some life domains that I hear moms wanting to prioritize:
+ Family
+ Friendships
+ Community
+ Spirituality
+ Personal growth
+ Education and learning
+ Culture
+ Nature

- Health
- Fitness
- Play / Leisure
- Rest
- Career
- Contribution
- Finances

Getting clear on your essentials will help you to strongly prioritize these and empower you to say no to the excess or unnecessary. How? You'll have greater clarity on what your main areas of focus are and what is not. This then will free up your energy, time and space for what matters most to you. But remember, first, above all, we must be crystal clear on what is most important and why.

Get comfortable pausing and asking yourself questions when offers, requests or things vying for your attention come up. Like:

- Will this request to take on another day back at the office give me more time for my top priorities or take me away from them?
- If I say yes to the invite to a playdate with another mom and her baby, will this align with my priorities or lead me further away from them?

There is no right or wrong. It is all about getting clear on what is most important to you and working to prioritize that.

A useful exercise
Take ten minutes to sit down in a quiet spot. Take yourself

back to the ideal life you created for your future in the previous chapter. Notice what your priorities are in this future. How are you choosing to spend your time and energy and who with? Move through an ideal day. Notice what the vibrant you is concentrating her time on. Write these elements down. Keep this list somewhere you can see it daily and begin prioritizing these with each decision that you make.

HER STORY

JO, A PLUGGED-IN MAMA OF TWO

Jo is 36-years-old with two girls Willow, who is 4-years-old and Denver, who is 1-year-old.

HER VISION

When she added it up, she realized she was spending a couple of hours throughout her day scrolling social media. It was a time-consuming habit that she did not want to take with her into her future.

Jo also didn't want to spend as much time as she currently was on driving Denver to various activities and Willow to preschool. She started thinking about possibly dropping back to having her kids enrolled in only one activity per week and to ask her husband to do the preschool drop off and pick up a couple of days each week.

This gave her a little more time to spend baking – something she loved to do but never had time for in her current lifestyle.

Jo was happy with how much time she was spending with her kids and happy to keep the playdates in her schedule since these were a great time for her to catch up with the other moms.

HER ACTION

Jo and her husband had loved going for walks together but had stopped since having the kids. She realized that they could start going for walks once a week with Denver in the carrier when Willow was at preschool. Their one-year-old would either doze off or be entertained by the changing scenery so they could have an uninterrupted conversation! They even started holding hands – something that they hadn't done in years. It seemed like a simple and manageable shift but helped both of them to feel more connected and supportive of each other and they began remembering that they actually liked each other!

HER NOW

Simple shifts in Jo's schedule that prioritized aspects of her life that brought her joy – baking, spending time with mom friends and time outside with her husband – set her up for success as a vibrant mama.

Ask yourself what you can start changing in your day-to-day living to get more aligned with what is most important to you.

Prioritizing yourself can make for a better world

There is one more important thing to think about. I ask that you let your mind be free to think BIG for this one, without limitations and self-doubt.

How would you shape the world if overwhelm and depletion were no longer an issue for you?

What impact do you dream about having on your community or the world?

Prioritizing yourself also allows you to have a positive impact through meaningful work or contributions outside of yourself and your family too. I might be biased but I believe moms can create the most amazing communities, world and change the future for the better.

People and the planet need more moms freed from depletion so they can live life fully and with more purpose. Imagine if more world leaders and CEOs were empowered, energized mothers? What a world we would live in! I believe there would be more future-oriented decisions made, less focus on power and control and more value placed on harmony, health and cooperation.

What exciting, innovative, meaningful projects would you create if you had the energy? It might be beautiful music for others to enjoy, opening an eco-friendly shop, going back to your job as a lawyer, raising kids who value kindness or creating a documentary on the drawbacks of fast fashion.

Anything is possible when you see the power in prioritizing. Prioritize yourself, get your energy back and dream big. Your kids and the world will be a better place for it!

YOUR NEXT STEPS

Hopefully, this chapter has persuaded you that you need to prioritize yourself for the benefit of everyone. My hope for you is that you are starting to consider how you might go about reshuffling your life to better reflect your true priorities. Reading this book and doing the activities in each chapter is a great way to start! So congratulations, you're on your way!

The following will help clarify what matters most to you and motivate you to start prioritizing these:

Why prioritize you

Write down why prioritizing yourself would be a good thing for you, your family and the world at large. You are welcome to use the reasons outlined in this chapter and come up with some others that are unique to you.

Prioritize your relationship

Take a moment to recall a happy memory you shared with your part-ner. Notice what you are doing together and how you are treating and feeling toward your partner. Now focus on the future. Answer the following questions:

- What sort of relationship do you want to foster?
- How do you want to treat your partner?
- How do you want to talk to him?
- What activities do you want to be doing more of together?

Write down ways that you could foster more of this in your relation-ship right now and as you move into the future. Pick one tiny step to test out today.

Prioritize your big vision

- What are the key aspects of your life that are most important to you?
- What relationships and activities is your vibrant self focusing her time and energy on?

THINGS TO REMEMBER

Prioritize you – what does this even mean?

- Prioritizing yourself and your health is essential.
- If you put everyone else before you, you will eventually burn out and have nothing left to give others.
- Prioritizing yourself is best for your family too.
- It is so much easier to be the parent you want to be for your kids when you take care of yourself.

Prioritizing your partnership

- Taking time for your partnership allows you to model a healthy relationship for your little ones, makes it easier to show up as an engaged and mindful parent and you will feel more supported.
- It is useful to find supportive people outside of your marriage. It is too much pressure to expect our partners to be everything for us.
- Clear communication goes a long way to strengthening your relationships and it doesn't have to be complicated.
- Don't assume your partner can read your mind. They can't.
- Be kind to each other and practice saying sorry.

Prioritize your big vision

- Clarity about your priorities helps guide your choices, actions and how you spend your time and energy.

CHAPTER 4

CONFIDENCE

WHO ARE YOU REALLY AND WHAT MATTERS MOST TO YOU?

Values are like a north star that you can check in with to see if you are moving your life in the direction you want.

The value of values

On a trip back to Canada while pregnant with Oak, I went out for lunch with an old school friend, Tamara. Her mom joined us. They were both thrilled that I had a baby on the way. In Tamara's mom's excitement, she asked if I was going to settle down.

"Uh Mom! She's not settling down!" Tamara answered for me. The idea of settling down was off putting to both my friend and me. It felt constricting, boring or almost anti-feminist to us.

Once I was on the other side of the pregnancy with a baby, however, I suddenly understood why people buy the home, get the dog and then have kids – why they, for lack of a better term, *settle* down. While my life might have looked exciting with the epic beaches, travel adventures, and expat lifestyle I had, I was craving a simplicity and ease which it did not provide.

The idea of settling down quickly grew quite appealing and became surprisingly liberating in my mind. Adventure had ranked very highly on my core values list for years. I lived by this value by exploring new places, moving often, making new friends in new places and saying yes when opportunities arose. But, with the arrival of my sweet baby boy, my values were changing as my priorities and life circumstances shifted.

As my motherhood journey continued, adventure no longer ranked so highly for me. Simplicity moved up the list while others like contribution, connection, kindness and health continued to rank highly. Yet the choices I made were not moving toward a life of ease. I was still living a life of adventure. For goodness sake, I agreed to a six-month caravan road trip around Australia when I was pregnant with Moss and had a 20-month-old Oak in tow. And that was after travelling overseas three times and moving house twice since Oak had been born. I look back now and wonder how I did that – and *why* I did it.

The answer was because adventure was still very exciting for my husband and it was his valuing of this that drove that trip. I didn't have the clarity at that time to understand that adventure was no longer as important to me and that what I really wanted my life to be about was simplicity, connection with others and health as I prepared to bring our second baby into the world.

Living my life by the misaligned value of adventure was exhausting and started to feel inauthentic. It was so useful for me to revisit my core values and question these. For too long I had lived according to an outdated list of my core values, values defined by my younger self for a different time of life. No wonder I felt burnt out! I needed to start living aligned with a revised version of my value system. Once I clarified this for myself, it was so much easier to make decisions that supported me in becoming healthier and happier while bringing more of what I wanted into my life.

I talked about this change within myself and this shift in my values to Luke. He gets it. We've communicated clearly about it. In fact, he is the one to pull me up when I start letting other less important values guide my decisions. Every day I am bringing more simplicity into my life because I am choosing to embody my values. You can too!

Connecting with values leads to confidence

In my therapeutic work with clients, values have always played a central role. Values are like a north star that you can check in with to see if you are moving your life in the direction you want to at any given moment.

I've witnessed the confidence that comes when clients connect with their values and use these to guide their choices, actions and life. Suddenly the overwhelm and indecision fall away, and they know what they want. Embracing values shifts how they treat themselves and how they show up in the world. A transformation is more possible when you identify what type of person you want to be. You begin using this to make choices and doing things that are meaningful for you.

What to expect in this chapter

We will begin this chapter by getting clear on *why* you want to get yourself out of exhaustion and *why* you want to make a better life. Then we will move into clarifying your values. We will end by tying this together into a simple mission statement.

There is an assured energy that comes from knowing what is most important to you and what qualities you want your life to be centred around. You are less likely to get caught up in people pleasing, trying to live up to other's expectations or trying to do everything for everyone when your values are clearly defined.

Instead, you will show up more authentically as you. Your choices, the way you behave, and the shape your life takes will move you in the direction of meaning if you let your values be your guide.

FIND YOUR *WHY*

First, let's clarify *why* you want to be vibrant. Why even bother moving towards this desired future you envisioned in Chapter 2? Why bother getting yourself out of burnout and into a more uplifting place?

You have started getting clear on *what* it is that you want, so now it is time to start asking *why*.

It can be all too easy to stay stuck in exhaustion, irritability and moodiness. There is something sickly satisfying about wallowing and feeling a bit sorry for yourself. I have been there – just ask my husband!

I remember days when I was sulky and quick to snap at anything Luke said. I had thoughts like, "I am alone in this" and "It is all too hard." I knew that getting some exercise outside in the fresh air or talking to a friend about how I was feeling would help. On those days I could have so easily stayed indoors, not given myself a break from the kids and let the negative spiral continue. Picturing what I wanted for my future and the future of my family was a good first step to getting me out of these funks and prioritizing myself.

However, it wasn't until I got clear on *why* I wanted to make changes to the direction my life was going that I made up my mind to take myself and my wellness seriously.

It all starts with asking *why*...
In my clinical work, I have used plenty of tools that help my clients dive deeper into their psyche. One of the simplest strategies is asking the same question on repeat till they get to the real meaning within. It is like peeling an onion and slowly finding more layers and depth. In the end, what you find is usually something quite simple at its core.

You can do this with fears, beliefs and just about anything. I like asking *why* to get to the core of well, *why*, you want what you want. Knowing your *why* gives what you are working towards a much greater meaning – and a stronger foundation to work from. That is essential if you want to stay motivated when the excitement of making a change wears off (and it will). Having a simple, meaningful reason to come back to can help you keep moving toward your vibrant future. It can ensure longevity of your new habits.

Not long after realizing that I needed clarity about my own life, I turned this therapeutic questioning technique on myself.

Asking *why* came to me one day as I played with Oak on the living room floor. So, I sat there on the playmat that day surrounded by his toys and the unfinished housework and opened my journal. I began asking myself *why*.

Why do I want to move toward this vibrant future me?
Because I am so sick of being tired and want to be energetic again.

Why?
Because I want to feel like myself again.

Why?
Because I want to do the things that I love to do and enjoy my life and motherhood.

Why?
Because I want to be a great mom who is attuned, engaged, playful, kind and healthy. I want to be a role model for my kids, and have a positive impact on my kids, others and the planet that they are growing up in.

Why?
Because I want my kids to be as healthy and happy as possible and make positive contributions to the planet and other people throughout their lives too.

Asking *why* five times clarified a lot for me. I wanted to have the energy to do the things that would make me the best mom

I could be so I could raise my kids to be happy, healthy and positive influences on others and the planet. Uncovering my core reason translated into motivation that will keep me moving forward and improving upon my goal when the going gets tough. Knowing my *why* gave my goal purpose, which is a lot more motivating than simply saying, "Because I want to feel more energetic."

Something switched in my brain and thought process after exploring my *whys*. I realized that being a strong role model for my kids and being engaged, attuned and playful with them was far more important than trying to convince myself and others that I am a "supermom" who can do everything herself.

Raising healthy and happy kids who would care about others and the planet was infinitely more important to me than ensuring that I had a spotless house that I had cleaned myself from top to bottom.

Being able to show up for myself to do the work I am passionate about was so much more important and motivating than trying to be everything to everyone.

It was only after accessing my *why* that I was able to admit that I was failing at being "super mom," failing at keeping my house sparkling clean all the time and failing at living up to society's expectations of what a *good mom* is "supposed to be." And once that came up for myself, what I felt was relief. I had been trying to live and operate as a mother by toxic expectations instilled in me by external forces – and I was finally breaking free of them. And I was starting to let go of self-expectations too.

An example of letting go of an expectation

By this point, I hope that you can better identify external expectations, but it's important as well to recognize that we all create self-expectations too. These can confuse our ideal life vision if we're not mindful. Self-expectations can be harmful too.

For myself, I was failing at living up to my own green living expectations. Since I am passionate about the environment, I unconsciously set myself rigid expectations, like I needed to have my kids in cloth diapers all of the time and if I used disposables (even if they were biodegradable and made of bamboo) I would be found out and declared a fraud eco mama. I also put relentless pressure on myself to make all of my kids' food, baby wipes and cleaning products, even though it was exhausting me and there were amazing, healthy alternatives available in my local shops.

It was powerful to uncover why being an eco-mama was important to me. Equally powerful was discovering the faulty and rigid expectations I had of what an eco-mama was. This made it so much easier to let these self-expectations go alongside doing all these eco-tasks myself. And to let them go without guilt. I began asking for help with what I couldn't or didn't want to do. I began using eco-resources from local shops to cut down on my workload, so that I could have more time in my day.

Outsourcing – what a concept!

Empowered by my *why*, I began asking directly for more help in other areas of my life too – and not feeling guilty about it. I asked Luke to take over specific tasks like getting Oak changed in the morning. We had an honest conversation about scheduling, and he stopped working his weekly 24-hour shift so he could be home more evenings. I hired a cleaner. I sourced the best disposable diapers I could find (yes, they were still biodegradable) for use when we were out of the house and overnight. I even sought the guidance of a naturopath and osteopath to speed up my journey back to health.

These shifts in support freed me. I was able to devote a little more energy to what mattered most to me. I began going for walks in nature by myself. I delved further into my studies on nutrition and environmental medicine. I got back to my psychology roots and started writing more often about raising healthy and happy kids. I even started applying what I was writing about to my own family life. I was no longer running on empty but instead had more energy to be more fun with my family.

What is your why? And why?
Take a moment and ask yourself *why* you want to be a vibrant mom. Ask *why* after you come up with your response. Go through this at least five times – but go further if that works for you. Don't overthink what you write down – answer as the thoughts and feelings emerge. Notice what comes up for you.

Do this privately so other people's opinions don't muddle your answers. You have to let go of defences, expectations and societal norms. Instead, connect with your intuition. Otherwise, the *whys* that you come up with will have little real meaning to you. You know at a gut level if you are being honest with yourself. Go there. Write it all down. This will become part of your mission statement which you will get into shortly.

VALUES - WHO DO YOU WANT TO BE?

Values help you to clarify what is worthwhile and meaningful to you. They are what you consider to be most important in the way you live your life – the qualities you aim to embody. Knowing your values will make it easier to make decisions, to know how you want to act, how you want to treat yourself, your kids and others, and what you want to focus your time on. Who are you committed to being?

Values are guides to help you make decisions that give you purpose, fulfilment and help move you in the direction of becoming a vibrant mama – whatever that specifically looks like to you. Alternatively, when you make decisions or take actions that are misaligned with your values, you will likely find yourself frustrated, unsatisfied or disappointed. You might find yourself still stuck in burnout or slipping back into its depths.

Think of your values as your guiding principles. They are there to remind you of who you want to be and how you want to show up in the world. They are your guide you as you make decisions, move through your day and create your reality.

Here is an example. Since health is one of my key values, I am satisfied and happy when I choose a healthy meal at a café. Whereas, if I picked a heavy and fried option, not only would I feel lethargic afterwards, but I would also be frustrated with myself. Deep fried meals aren't aligned with my values. They don't move me closer to the healthy, energetic person I want to be, but instead move me further away from this.

Here are a few examples of values to get you thinking: simplicity, affection, clarity, compassion, health, authenticity, gratitude, contribution, curiosity, efficiency, honesty, adventure, fun, autonomy, love, optimism, growth, and creativity – but there is an endless number of possible values out there.

Values are not goals

Values are the quality of how and what you do, whereas goals are the actions you take. A fulfilling life can be found in living by your values, not simply by ticking your goals off a list. They also aren't morals or priorities, but ways of being.

My core values will be different from yours and that is okay and to be expected. They aren't what you think you should do or what you think others would want you to value – they must be authentic to you. Get clear on what matters to you; not what you think your mother-in-law, your mom friends or boss expects of you. There are no values that are better or worse than others, some are simply more important to you than they would be to somebody else. Also, your values can and often do change over time. Thus, it is helpful to revisit a value setting exercise a couple of times throughout the year to clarify which values are currently top of mind for you.

Getting married and becoming a mother are goals. You can have a wedding and tick getting married off your goal list. You can get pregnant and birth a child. Values on the other hand are the characteristics that you want to embody. For example, you might value being a kind and loving mother. These aren't things you can do once and be done with. Kindness and love are ways of being that you can choose to bring to any moment.

The cool thing about values is that while they can't be achieved, they are always available to you. Even if you don't act aligned with a value in one moment, you are able to reconnect with it in the next if you so choose.

I will note that despite values being incredibly important to guide your choices, habits and life, they are not something to adhere to in a rigid and unyielding fashion. Hold your values lightly and recognize that other people may have vastly different values that they prioritize – and that is fine. We are all free to choose what is most important to each of us and yours too will shift as times goes.

How to Clarify Your Values Exercise
Clarifying your values is a critical step to gaining clarity about what you want your life to be about.

So make yourself a warm tea. Grab your notebook. And find the quietest spot in your house – the one that makes you feel calm and safe. As you go through this section, note down any values that come to mind. I also recommend taking some time afterwards to sit and let your mind consider the way you want to show up for yourself, your children and in life in general. This is a process, so it is helpful to do this exercise a few times over a couple of weeks to get super clear on what values are key for you. And a reminder once again – getting caught up in other people's expectations is easy, so be wary that those aren't sneaking into your values.

Cast your mind forward into the future that supports you in being vibrant. Take a moment to settle into the scene of a typical day in this desired future. Now, let's get clear on how the best version of you shows up in this life.

Here's how. Remember to take as long as you want with this. As you come out of it, write down some of the key values that came to mind.

Step 1:

First, take your mind to your children. Imagine they are playing nearby. They don't realize that you can hear them, and they are talking about you. How would you like them to describe you? How are they describing how you act toward them? Get specific on what qualities you ideally want them to see in you. Consider what qualities you want to instil in them during their early years.

Step 2:

Stay in this vibrant future a little longer. Take your mind to a scene where your partner, friends, colleagues and extended family are. They too are talking about you. What would you like to hear them saying about you? Pay attention to what characteristics and qualities they see in this vibrant version of you.

Step 3:

Now go within. Consider how this future you treat herself? What qualities does she see in herself?

If further clarification is needed

If you are still a bit stuck on finding your values, consider the following questions. Write down whatever comes to mind. It doesn't matter if you write down three or fifteen qualities.

- How would I like others to describe me?
- How would I like to describe myself?
- How would I like my kids to describe me when they look back on their childhood?
- When am I my best possible self. What qualities do I exude?
- In an ideal world, where I do not struggle with stress, fear of judgement, exhaustion, anger, self-doubt, or any other uncomfortable emotion or thought, what qualities do I focus on fostering in myself?
- What qualities do I want to inspire in my children?
- What attributes do I respect in others?

Review honestly

Go through your list. See if you can narrow your list down to ten or less. Then challenge yourself to pick your top 3-5. Write these down somewhere you will see them often, tell a friend or write about why these are important to you right now. Remind yourself regularly of your key values.

Keep your key values top of mind

I often remind myself of my core values in the morning upon waking. I find this five second check-in is a simple way to orient the decisions I make and the actions I take each day to be aligned with what is important to me. Adding a new habit can be easy if you attach it to a current habit. For instance, you could add a values check-in to the end of a gratitude practice or meditation, to when you are brushing your teeth or waiting for the kettle to boil. Or just put a prompt in your phone to go off every morning at a specific time to remind you.

Determine how and when you will check in with your values daily to make it as easy as possible for you to consistently do so. By doing so, your choices and behaviour will begin to be made from this vibrant you instead of from the current overextended, tired or frazzled you.

AUTHENTIC YOU ANCHOR

This is a personal mission statement. It is a useful tool to quickly refer back to in trying times or when you are unclear about what the best move forward is. Don't worry, this isn't another 'to do' item – you've already done the bulk of the work by defining your value system. Creating a mission statement based on your *why*, core values and priorities can help you to use these to guide what you choose and do daily.

Once you are clear on your values and mission, you can share this with your partner so they understand what your decisions are based upon and can support you to live by this. They may even want to make their own. Also, it can be amazing to create a family mission statement with your partner and as your children get older, they can be contributors to this too.

Your Anchor You Anchor Guide

Feel free to write your mission statement however you like but if you want a simple structure to guide you, here's one to start with:

My intention is to live in a way that makes me feel _____, _____ and _____, so that I have time and space to be _____, _____ and _____ (based on your five *whys*).

My key values _____, _____ and _____ help guide my choices and actions to make it easier for me to show up as the person I want to be for _____, _____, and _____ (your top priorities).

HER STORY:

MAMA MARGOT

Here is an example of a mission statement that a client of mine, Margot, put together. Her key values were fun, caring and contribution. She went deep on her *why* and she had already gotten clear on her priorities which were herself, her marriage, her kids and her community.

HER VISION

So, she put together the following value-based mission statement:

"My intention is to be a role model for my daughters to see that women can have fun, be kind and also have a meaningful impact on those around them. My key values, fun, caring and contribution help guide my choices and actions to make it easier for me to show up as the person I want to be for myself, my marriage, my kids and to have a positive impact in my community."

HER ACTION

Margot found that her mission statement was a good reminder when making decisions, both big and small. For instance, when she went to buy a new toy for her daughters, she considered whether she thought they would find it fun (playful); if it was ethically made (caring for others and the planet) and if by purchasing she was making a positive contribution (buying local to support small businesses in her community).

Move forward with further confidence

In this chapter, you gained more clarity on what you want your life to be about. You are now clear on *why* you want to be a vibrant mom and what your values are. With these, you have created a simple personal statement that you can use to remind yourself of why you do what you do, make choices with ease and confidence, and embody your version of the vibrant mama more effortlessly.

YOUR NEXT STEPS

Now it is your turn to get clear on your big *why*, your core values and mission statement.

Find your why

Ask yourself 'Why do I want to be a vibrant mom?' and continue asking why to each answer you come up with. Ask why at least five times.

- Why do I want to be a vibrant mom?
- Why?
- Why?
- Why?
- Why?

The more whys you ask and answer, the more depth you can see. This is how you discover what truly matters to you at the core.

Your values

Answer the following questions to get you starting in clarifying your values (aka guiding principles) with that future you in mind:

- What qualities do I want my decisions, actions and life to be about?
- When I am my best possible self, what qualities will I exude?
- What qualities do I want to inspire in my children?

Look over your list and pick the top values that stick out for you. Write these down somewhere visible so you can be reminded of them regularly.

Check in with these values throughout your day and week, and notice whether you are living in alignment with your core values in those moments.

Authentic you anchor

Create your personal mission statement by completing the following for yourself or making yours by combining your why, core values and key priorities together in your own way.

My intention is to live in a way that makes me feel _____,

_____ and _____, so that I have time and space to

be _____, _____ and _____ (based

on your five *whys*).

My key values _____, _____ and _____ help guide

my choices and actions to make it easier for me to show up

as the person I want to be for _____, _____, and

_____ (your top priorities).

THINGS TO REMEMBER

Your why

- It takes effort to make changes so knowing why you want to be energetic and happy will sustain you when motivation starts to drop.
- Knowing why you want to move out of burnout and live a more uplifting life will keep you motivated and on track.

Who do you want to be?

- Values are your guiding principles that help you move in the direction you want your life to go.
- Living aligned with your values makes for an authentic and fulfilling life.
- Authentic you anchor: This personal mission statement incorporates your priorities, why and values
- It helps to guide your choices and moves you closer to being the best version of yourself.

CHAPTER 5

CLARITY

WHY IT'S OKAY TO HAVE NEEDS AND EVEN MORE OKAY TO FULFIL THEM

Emotions are data that if you look at more closely, can tell you a lot about what is important to you and what you need.

Needs are natural

In the early days of mothering, I drastically lost touch with my own needs. Everything was about what Oak needed. I was always tuning into his emotions and looking for the need behind his behaviour. Why was he fussing? Was he hungry, tired, needing cuddles or a diaper change?

I temporarily forgot to check in with myself. I got caught up in my frustration, fatigue and overwhelm instead of being curious about these emotions and what they were trying to tell me. The result? Internal emotional havoc.

It wasn't until I learned how to gently take care of myself as

I would my child that I was able to parent more intentionally and calmly. Once my priorities had shifted back to myself, I was better able to tend to my needs. I started listening to my emotions again instead of just letting them run wild. Honestly, it felt rusty at first but in time I started picking up on my emotions much faster and figuring out what unmet needs might be hiding there before my feelings erupted. And once I mastered that internal dialogue, it was so much easier to articulate what I was needing to other people.

I recall a specific moment when I was pushing the stroller up the big hill to our home as Moss napped (to this day it seems to be a trend that my kids nap while I walk). It was another hot summer day. Sweat dripped down my back as I chatted with my mom on the phone. She was telling me all the reasons that I should be excited about an upcoming move. Many times before I had told her that I was happy where I was, enjoying the stability of being in one place and that it wasn't the right time for me to make such a change. I was finally feeling healthy and energetic. I was finally getting back to doing work that I was super excited about. I had a nice, simple pattern to my weeks that worked for me. I was not desiring such a massive life change – even if Luke was.

As she told me about all the lovely benefits of moving, I interrupted her and said, "What I need from you is to listen to me and really hear me. While what you are saying is likely all true, in this moment I don't find it helpful to hear. I need you to understand that I am finding this hard and I want support from you."

I said so in a clear, kind and caring way. I know she was only telling me these things because she cared about me and wanted the best for me. She wanted me to be excited for the move; her intentions were good. I knew it was hard for her to see me sad, halfway across the world, and she was trying to change that. But what I needed from her was to just be with me and let me process what I was feeling without trying to change me. Immediately she understood and the conversation deepened. It was an incredibly connecting conversation that grew our relationship, even if it had started off with me feeling invalidated and unheard. And a side benefit was without her trying to change my emotions, I actually ended up much cheerier in the end.

This sort of conversation certainly hasn't always come easily for me and still doesn't always. But now that I am in tune with my emotions and looking for the data they are trying to give me, it is so much easier. It can be for you too. And once you're aware of this process, you'll be empowered to disarm even the best of intentions from others if in fact they are further stressing you out.

What to expect in this chapter

You got clear on what is holding you back in Chapter 1. Then you had a bit of fun in the second chapter looking into the future and imagining what it is that you want to move towards. After that, you recognized what you need to prioritize and what your values are. Now, in this chapter, you will get clear on your needs, emotional signals and emotions. This will move you another step closer to more joy, vitality and calm.

WHAT ARE NEEDS ANYWAY?

Firstly, there are basic needs for your wellbeing like sleep, water, nourishing food, exercise, time in nature and living in a healthy, safe place. Remember, these needs are basic human requirements NOT luxuries that count as 'me time'. I hear too many moms talk about their showers or tidying up without their little ones 'helping' being their leisure time or an indulgence. Yet their husbands shower every day (and don't classify it as leisure time) while still managing to find time to watch sports on tv or go to the golf course for leisure. Mamas, repeat after me, you deserve to have your basic needs met; they are not a luxury.

There is another tier of needs: psychological needs. These can be more complex. Psychological needs include emotional support, appreciation, connection, affection, respect, freedom, empathy, relaxation, shared responsibility, being heard or the need to let go of things like unhelpful beliefs, high expectations or identities no longer serving you.

These also are not luxuries and often can be much more challenging to meet than the more basic ones.

Moms in particular are so focused on being attentive to their children's needs that they often stop paying attention to their own. Getting back in touch with your needs, noticing which of your needs are unmet and finding ways to support yourself can massively move you out of burnout.

Once you are clear on what your unmet needs are, you can often meet them yourself or be in a better position to ask others for assistance.

For instance, when I notice that I feel lonely and require connection, I can call up a good friend for a chat to fulfil the need for companionship. If I notice that I am exhausted and in need of rest, I can ask my husband to take the kids to the park so I can go and take a nap and satisfy my need for sleep. If I am irritable and realize that I haven't spent much time in nature lately, I can go outside to take the edge off.

Getting in touch with your needs makes it so much easier to get them met without huge emotional meltdowns, arguments or even much energy. It really does make life easier and help to keep your energy tank full.

Identify your needs, notice when they are being neglected and then ask yourself, how could I get this need met? Can I do so myself or do I need to ask for support from someone?

CLARIFY YOUR EMOTIONS

Let's take a step back from needs and look at emotions for a moment, because they are our signals that show us unmet needs. No emotion is good or bad, even if some are easier to experience than others. All emotions are just experiences. They are data that if you look at more closely, can tell you a lot about what is important to you and what you need.

Much of the time we don't bother to notice and acknowledge what it is that we are feeling. By ignoring this simple, but critical, step of awareness, we stay stuck in our emotional storm much longer and often react in ways we aren't very proud of. And we also miss out on the useful information that our emotions are trying to tell us.

We can often be tempted to define ourselves by the emotions we experience but you are not your emotions. I'm guessing you have said something like...

"I'm sad."

"I'm angry."

"I'm so overwhelmed."

"I'm exhausted."

"I'm anxious."

"I'm depressed."

I certainly have! While it may seem nit-picky to focus on the semantics here, the way we choose to use our words can play a big role in how we understand ourselves and deal with our emotions. Saying, "I am frustrated" is *defining* yourself as a frustrated person. However, frustration is an emotion that like all emotions, is a temporary state you can find yourself in. An emotional state isn't forever. All emotions come and go. They are not who you are.

Simply shifting the phrase, "I am lonely" to "I feel lonely" or "I feel lonely in this moment" separates you from the emotion. It empowers you. No longer are you defined by being lonely; you are not a lonely person all of the time. You are just experiencing loneliness right now. It is no longer permanent or personal.

You can go a step further in this mindset exercise by adding in:

"*A part of me is feeling lonely right now.*"

"*I am noticing that a part of me is feeling lonely right now.*"

Suddenly this emotion is no longer a permanent trait that you have, it is temporary, and you are the one that is observing it, not just experiencing it or living by it. This shift in wording can open up so much space between you and your emotions and allow you to feel them without trying to fight them.

Suppressing emotion hurts
Fighting, suppressing or avoiding emotions is a sure-fire way to keep them frequently coming back with a vengeance. It is exhausting to fight them and futile. Suppressing emotions is not helpful. It amplifies the distressing emotions you are trying to avoid. Suddenly these emotions are larger than life and your rational thinking brain shuts off. This is when you might yell at your kids, slam the door on your partner or cycle into a miserable heap on the floor.

Luckily, by taking a few seconds to notice how you are feeling and then label your emotion(s), you gain back some control of yourself. This simple (but not always easy) skill can help to reduce some of the intensity of your emotions. Also, when you are aware of what you are feeling you can more easily choose how to respond – instead of just letting the emotions drive your reactions.

Being able to understand and express emotions helps dramatically to reduce their hold over our behaviour. Most of us can improve our ability to understand and label our emotions. It might seem insignificant, but it is one of the greatest skills we can develop and teach our children. Not only does putting words to how we are feeling make it easier to express these emotions in healthy, adaptive ways, but it is associated with pretty much any positive outcome that we want for our kids (and ourselves) including succeeding at school and in the workplace, strong friendships, lasting relationships, robust mental health and even physical health. Trust me, I wrote my Ph.D. thesis on the subject![26,27]

As moms, our kids need us to be attuned with our emotions so they can learn to do the same with their own. Our children look to us for lessons in how to deal with their emotions. The most profound way for us to teach our little ones this is for us to model good emotional regulation – that is noticing our emotions, identifying them and expressing them appropriately.

Remember my spat with the toaster in a previous chapter? That's an example of poor emotional regulation – at the time I hadn't identified my emotions, so I didn't express them well. Instead, my emotions boiled over, and I went to battle with a kitchen appliance, and then my husband, which is not my proudest moment.

All in all, allow your emotions to exist, but create some distance from them by using intentional word choices to label whatever you're feeling. Doing so suddenly makes your emotions less overwhelming or scary. They become easier to navigate once they are clearly identified. Like a wave in the ocean, emotions too will come in, peak and dissipate. Emotions generally only last for 90 seconds if you actually allow them to be there. 90 seconds! That's it! After that, you actually have a lot more choice and control over how you respond to your emotions and circumstances. Suddenly it feels a lot more manageable to experience any emotion, doesn't it?[28]

Practice out loud

If you start using this technique, it will change your relationship with your emotions for the better. Practice it out loud. Let your kids hear it (even if they are only babies right now). They will soak it in and from a young age, they will have a much healthier relationship with their emotions as a result.

How do you start honing this essential skill? It's pretty simple to begin! Throughout your day, notice the different feelings that come up for you. Be curious about your emotions. Notice them. Name them. Ask yourself where you feel them in your body. What sensations are connected to the emotion? Create some space for the emotions to be there. Take a moment to put words to them.

"I'm feeling..."

"I notice I am experiencing the emotion of..."

"I notice a part of me is feeling..."

Here is a little example of what this could look like. Instead of:

"This laundry is so annoying!"

Try this:

"I notice I am feeling frustrated and angry when I look at the laundry pile."

"I notice that a part of me is feeling irritated and bitter."

"I notice my jaw is clenched and my shoulders are tense."

"I think I need to ask for some help with all the housework."

When we can identify and name our emotions, it is much easier to then express ourselves in healthy ways. And when you are in tune with your emotions it is way easier to get clear on what your needs are and therefore seek solutions. Almost always, when we are feeling really upset and out of alignment, it can be connected to an unmet need.

Start paying attention to your emotions, because they can guide you to a solution for finding and mending unmet needs.

EMOTIONS GIVE US INSIGHT INTO OUR UNMET NEEDS

Practice expressing your emotions, asking for help or finding ways to meet your needs yourself. A lot of the time, once you notice and name your own emotions and needs, you'll feel calmer. Expressing these appropriately can add yet another layer of calm. Then asking for support or finding ways that you can meet your needs yourself is the icing on the cake.

For myself, I notice feeling easily irritated and stressed when I haven't been consistently moving my body. Not enough physical activity and my body starts to feel heavy with agitation. These emotions and bodily sensations are there to remind me that I need to get out for a walk or do some yoga. And when I listen to what these feelings are telling me, I can better pull myself off the couch and go out for a hike, which restores by sense of calm.

Think about what signals your emotions and bodily sensations give you when you are needing sleep or food (ever felt hangry?!) What about when you feel unsupported by your partner or are failing to live up to your high expectations of yourself?

As you build these awareness skills and get to know your patterns well, knowing what you need and figuring out how to meet these needs for yourself isn't very hard all of a sudden.

What to do with challenging emotions

When you notice yourself feeling an uncomfortable emotion, like frustration, stress, sadness or shame, get in the habit of asking yourself, "What do I need?" You may not know straight away, but over time you will be able to more quickly and easily identify what is missing and more readily seek out support.

However, our brains don't work their best when we are highly emotional – like when you are feeling full blown rage or on the floor hysterically crying. So that may not be the time to challenge yourself to figure out what your unmet needs are. Instead, in these moments simply label what you are feeling, allow the emotions to come and go, and treat yourself as kindly as possible.

Once the emotional storm has subsided and you can think more clearly again, consider what you may have needed. The following questions can be useful to ask yourself at this time:

- What could I have done to help myself not get to such an intense place?
- What did I need?
- What were my emotions screaming out to me about?
- What were these emotions trying to tell me?

Emotional states in relation to unmet needs

Here is a list of a few feelings or states that are often linked to unmet needs. Consider how relevant these are to you and add to the list from your own unique experience. By no means is this list complete, applicable or exact for everyone. One mama may need more connection with others when they are sad, whereas another may prefer space to be alone in these times. What is important is to get clear on what you are feeling and needing personally.

- **Overwhelm** – Needing support (this support could come in many different forms depending on what your unique situation is), needing to do less (stop doing some things, delegate, ask for help, involve others.
- **Exhaustion** – Needing rest, sleep, relaxation, empathy, to do less and have more support.
- **Loneliness** – Needing connection, love, affection, time in nature.
- **Self-doubt** – Needing to connect with your strength and intuition.
- **Anger** – Needing to clarify and assert your boundaries.

- **Resentment** – Needing appreciation and acknowledgement, needing more shared responsibility with your partner.
- **Rejection** – Needing connection to others and community.
- **Frustration** – Needing me time, needing more time to do the things that bring you joy or purpose.
- **Jealousy** – Needing self compassion, needing to refocus on gratitude and find clarity about what shifts you can make to create the life you desire for yourself.
- **Unmotivated** – Needing to take a break or rest, change focus or connect with your values and priorities.
- **Stress** – Needing support, needing to let go of unhelpful, high expectations, possibly needing some of your health non-negotiables (e.g., sleep, food, movement, time in nature) assessed.
- **Irritability** – Needing more time in nature, movement and likely a check in with all health non-negotiables, needing more support.
- **Anxiety** – Needing emotional support (reassurance and empathy), connection, gentle guidance, to come back to the present moment, gratitude, connection with your intuition, safety.
- **Guilt** – Needing to apologize; needing connection, and a reminder of your priorities, values and how you want to show up in the world.
- **Sadness** – Needing emotional support, connection to others, empathy.
- **Confusion** – Needing connection, reassurance, support,

rest, breaks, simplicity, more time to do the things that bring you joy or purpose.

Start asking yourself, "What am I feeling and what do I need in this moment?" Listen to what your body tells you. The body often knows what it is that you need. Slow down and pay attention.

Also keep in mind that needs are not always about needing more. A lot of the time they can be about doing less. Less people pleasing. Less housework. Less filling your schedule with busyness. Less time scrolling social media and other drains. Embracing the idea of doing less will help to counter any people-pleasing tendencies you might have and start establishing healthy boundaries so you can honour your value system, emotional state and needs.

What do you need to say no thank you to?

CLEARLY COMMUNICATE NEEDS

Even if no one is around other than your baby or toddler, it can be powerful for you say out loud how you are feeling and what you need. Imagine you are in a rush to leave the house and your little one is not cooperating – this is a daily occurrence, right mamas? One option is to let the frustration build and then end up exhausted in a heap no further ahead or losing your temper with your kiddos. Another option is to talk it through with your little one, even if they are way too young to understand the words you are using. Such as:

"Mommy is feeling very frustrated and impatient right now. I

would appreciate if you would cooperate with me to get dressed."

Your little one may not understand what you are saying or be able to get themselves dressed, but that is not the point. The point is you noticing, naming and expressing how you are feeling and what you need before getting snippy. This has been a game changer for me. Instead of emotions and thoughts whirling around in your head, this simple exercise helps clarify how you feel and what you need. It is useful to use with other adults too or even when alone. For example:

"I notice I am feeling sad and lonely. What I need right now is to get outside into the sunshine, get some exercise and talk to a friend. So, I am going to push my baby in the stroller down to the local café for a cup of tea and call a friend for a chat as I go."

Initially, you might feel silly talking to yourself, but I promise, you will actually feel a lot better by doing so. Think of it like a scene from a movie – you are the main character having a little self-monologue. You will feel in control of your actions and you won't get completely caught up in your emotions. In turn, you will more easily realize what it is you need in the moment. And most of the time you can help yourself get these needs met yourself or by being clear with others about what you want.

This technique is great to use with your partner too. Remember what we talked about earlier – they are not mind readers, as much as we may wish they were. We need to clearly communicate how we are feeling, what we need and how they can help us. Most of the time they want to be helpful and supportive but don't necessarily know where to start. Let's make it easy for them to make life a little easier for us. For example:

"I notice a part of me is feeling resentful when I am home alone for most of the day with the kids. I need to split some of the chores and time caring for the kids a bit more evenly with you. I would love some support from you on this, specifically, if you could come home a bit earlier so I can have some time to myself. Would that work for you?"

It is useful when communicating the need for more support in an area to offer an idea or two to your partner which would help remedy the situation. Simply stating your emotions, needs and what you want with more clarity can help you get needs met that you cannot meet yourself. This practice takes intention and practice but is doable. When I do this, I save my energy for more important things like having fun with my family instead of wasting it on more emotional anguish.

What would you prefer to spend your energy on?

HER STORY:

AMY, MAMA OF TWO

As we've been discussing in depth, moms are notorious for putting the needs of others before their own – often to the point of losing touch with what they need altogether. Amy was one such mom. She had always been very efficient, caring and capable in everything that she did. This filtered into her marriage and later into her family dynamics as they had children. She busied herself in keeping the house tidy. She did the lion's share of the child-rearing. She was happy for her husband, Paul, to sleep in a different room for the first few months so his sleep wasn't disrupted by their newborn's frequent wake-ups – never mind her sleep being disrupted several times each night.

HER STRUGGLE

She worked hard to keep the family happy, the house in order and life functioning. Amy managed juggling it all until she had her second child, Ava. Then it quickly started wearing her down. She was disregarding her own needs, like good sleep, getting adequate support, having more shared responsibility of household chores and child-rearing with her husband, appreciation and time to herself, over and over to meet her family's.

It all hit her one day. Her three-year-old, Henry was begging her to play with him, but she was tidying up the kitchen while holding Ava in one arm. Then he said quietly, "You never play with me. You love Ava more." She felt like she had been punched in the stomach. She already felt so guilty that she wasn't able to be as fun and light-hearted with Henry or spend as much one-on-one time with him anymore. But she hadn't realized the impact it had had on him. She was just too tired and busy trying to stay on top of everything else.

HER ACTION

Amy began connecting to her emotions and needs more. For instance, when Amy noticed she felt overwhelmed, she realized it was often because she didn't feel supported by her husband. In time she caught this pattern more quickly. She then started seeking support before she got totally sucked into a negativity spiral of yelling, resentment, anger and more overwhelm. This helped her to have more energy left over to connect with her little ones more.

Amy also started asking for help from her extended family, taking more time for herself and dividing chores more evenly with her husband. It took them some time, some super clear communication and Amy committing to getting her own needs met along with everyone else's, but they have worked out the kinks. Not only does she feel calmer, but her guilt and anger have eased too. She feels more liberated and excited to play with her little ones as she doesn't have quite as much on her plate anymore.

HER NOW

It took some time for Paul to adjust. He was used to Amy doing so much and suddenly he was having to step up. He was shocked to find out how much she had been doing. Step by step, however, they found a new joint rhythm together that more equally divided the tasks of parenthood and created more space for Amy to fulfil her needs.

Keep tabs on your emotional state

In this chapter, you became aware of what needs you have and whether or not they are being met. Then you connected to your emotions. Finally, you explored ways to express your emotions simply to yourself and to others and find healthy ways to meet your unmet needs.

YOUR NEXT STEPS

Take some time to work through these exercises to get crystal clear on your emotions and needs.

Clarify your emotions
As you go about your day, pay attention to your emotions.

Ask yourself what emotion you are feeling, where you feel it in your body and what thoughts you are having.

Connect emotions and needs
After noticing your emotions, consider what unmet needs may be underlying these.

Brainstorm some simple ways of getting this need met by yourself or by asking for specific help from others.

Ask yourself the following questions:
- What am I feeling and what do I need in this moment?
- What do I need to ask for?
- What do I need to say no thank you to?

Clearly communicate needs
Practice stating your emotions, what you would like (your need) and asking for specific support. See what happens!

THINGS TO REMEMBER

So, what are needs?
- Basics needs are not a luxury but a requirement. These include

– but are not limited to – food, shelter, sleep, movement and a healthy environment.

* More complex needs are not indulgences either but they can be more difficult to meet. These include emotional support, connection, shared responsibility, appreciation, affection and relaxation.

Clarify your emotions

* Emotions are here to tell you about what is important to you and what you need.
* Suppressing emotions isn't helpful. It often intensifies the emotion you are trying to avoid.
* Getting clear on your emotions makes it easier to express them in healthy ways and is helpful for better relationships, career success and health.

Emotions give us insight into our unmet needs

* If you look closely at your emotions, you can often find unmet needs there.

Clearly communicate needs

* Practice expressing your emotions and asking for support with your unmet needs. In time it gets easier, emotions don't build up as much and you may just find yourself with a whole lot more of what you need.

CHAPTER 6

THRIVE

THE POWER OF LASTING TRANSFORMATION LIES IN YOUR DECISION MAKING

You shape your outer reality when you gain clarity on your inner world and intentionally make choices from this place.

Start simplifying your choices

Becoming a vibrant mama may feel like a daunting process, but at the end of the day it is simply a choice. It is up to you to choose to become her, to embody the vision of the ideal life you want to lead. It sounds simple right? It can be and in theory alone it should be, but if you're anything like me, making decisions have never been my strength. I needed to work on this mental muscle to fortify my dream of becoming the confident and content mama I had always imagined.

I had labelled myself as someone who struggles to make decisions for much of my life. I have wasted too much time pouring over the details of which stroller to buy, which mattress is the least toxic but affordable or where to send the kids once they were ready for *daycare*. Before becoming a mother, I drained my energy by to-ing and fro-ing with which style of dress to wear to my friend's wedding, which Airbnb to stay at when booking holidays and even what to order when out for dinner. I used to be terrified of picking the 'wrong' restaurant when going out with friends for fear of choosing poorly or disappointing others. I was the queen of analysis paralysis. It was exhausting.

As time passed, I have applied many of the therapeutic strategies I use in my work with clients to my own challenges, including decision making. Now I have incredible clarity on what I want, what supports me to be the best version of myself, and what I want my life to look like as a vibrant mama. In short, I empowered my choice to redefine the motherhood experience on my terms and I want to share that ability with you.

Bring clarity to your decision-making process

With this clarity, I now don't get as frazzled when making decisions. I simply ask myself what would the vibrant me choose here? What would she do in this situation? I make my decisions from this perspective instead of from the exhausted, overwhelmed, or uncertain place I may find myself in that specific moment. I know this vital version of myself so well because I visualize her in detail, I know my why, I understand my values, and I am connected to my needs and emotions. I embody her daily in the choices I make. I *choose* to be her.

I realized that if I made my choices from this future version of myself who prioritizes herself, lives aligned with her values, is attuned with her emotions, and finds ways to meet her needs in healthy ways, I would make better decisions for myself on the whole. Gosh, did it ever work! While I may never win a gold medal in decision making, I now make choices with so much more ease, efficiency and confidence. And these are all guided by myself intentionally, rather than from seeking the opinions of outside sources who think they know what is best for me.

Not only does it make decision making easier, but these decisions then move me closer to the life I want. Each decision, big or small, shifts me toward being calmer, happier, more playful and having more simplicity. It is pretty magical.

An example of what would the vibrant you do

One afternoon Moss was unsettled. I was tired and at my wits' end. My patience was wearing thin with him. I sat down on the couch as he clawed at me wanting attention I did not have. I considered turning the tv on to zone us both out and nearly did so. The shiny silver flatscreen called out to me temptingly.

But first I got in tune with how I was feeling (tired, stressed and frustrated) and my needs (needing more time for myself and the things I enjoy, aka needing to prioritize me). I reminded myself of my key values. In this case, the situation spoke to my value of being connected to the natural world.

I then asked myself, *"What would the vibrant me do here?"*

Zoning out in front of the tv while Moss continued to cry and fuss would have moved me away from being the mom, and the person, I want to be. (There is absolutely no judgement here if you love watching tv and it refreshes you. It just doesn't for me. If anything, it drains me further. This is yet another example of why we have to get clear on what works for us personally).

Okay, so what were my other options? While I was home alone, I couldn't get any time to myself at that specific moment. But I could prioritize my wellbeing and destress by getting out in nature, moving my body and clearing my mind with Moss in tow. A walk outside it was!

Even though in that moment, I most definitely wasn't feeling like going through the effort of getting outside, I knew it was the best decision for me. So, I strapped on the baby carrier, popped Moss in and walked out the door. Within two minutes, we were both feeling better. We were calmer and happier. Refreshed, Moss fell asleep and I gained my energy and optimism back. The mood of the day was saved because I took the time to check in with myself.

Choices are everywhere – choose wisely and in alignment with yourself

I had been faced with a decision, and in that moment, guided by the clarity I had of who I want to be, I made a helpful choice that moved me toward being my version of a vibrant mama. I chose vibrancy. I avoided the all too likely scenario of Luke coming home to not only Moss crying, but me too.

There is power in letting your values, needs and life vision guide you instead of allowing your mood, energy level or negative inner critic consume you. In other words, when you understand your *why*, your decisions are made from a place of inner confidence rather than confusion.

What to expect in this chapter

In this chapter, you will explore the practice of making intentional choices with grace. As you will soon see, decision making will become increasingly easier when you start to apply the clarity you have gained from your work thus far in earlier chapters. You have access to everything you need to make decisions that move you toward the vibrant mama you want to be. With every action you take, you are now able to create the life you want for yourself and your family. It is incredible to realize how much power each one of us has in every microshift we make. This is really exciting stuff!

BETTER DECISIONS ARE YOUR SUPERPOWER

It's time to do away with the "supermom" myth. It's toxic and harmful. The real superpower at play in the modern motherhood journey is being able to make decisions that are aligned with your values. And you are well on your way!

- You have taken time to imagine the sort of life you want for you and your family – one that supports you to be the vibrant mom you know you can be.
- You know the importance of needing to be your number one priority.
- You are getting clear on what it is that your values, needs and emotions are, and checking in with these daily.

All of these qualities, all of the work you've done up to this point, will inform the decisions you make.

Stepping out of burnout and into the vibrant mama you want to be takes more than clarity sitting in a notebook. You have to start using that clarity as an active tool to do things differently. That means making new choices and creating new habits that move you closer to what you want. It doesn't have to be hard, but you do have to be intentional and committed.

You can do this!

Now, of course, sometimes it will feel hard, no question. Establishing any new habit with longevity is. But the great thing is that you can do hard things. You are a mother. You have created, grown and birthed babies – and that's all before the hard work you put in once they were earth side. You *can* do amazing things! You already are! You don't have to make changes in super hard, huge ways. It is all about making little, consistent shifts, or microshifts, in your daily choices, routines, and mindset. It's about honing your decision-making superpower with the structure and techniques we've been exploring and developing in this book up to this point.

Be mindful of your decisions

As long as your decisions remain unconscious, you have little say in what you do or what direction your life goes in. You are at the peril of your habitual ways. Bringing awareness to your decisions and habits is needed to get out of default mode and consciously into intentional decision making that is aligned with your core values.

Begin noticing what is driving your choices.

Are these choices made without much thought and coming from where you are right now? Are they coming from fear, scarcity or guilt?

Or are you making your decisions intentionally and from the perspective of the future you who takes amazing care of herself, is in control of how she spends her time and what she focuses her energy on?

What you base your choices on creates the life you live one decision at a time. That's right, decisions are like little building blocks! What life are your choices creating for you?

What is a choice point?
A choice point is a moment in which we have the ability to act in ways that either take us *towards* or *away* from who we want to be, what we care about most and what we want our life to be about. Awareness is key at this point – it assists us to make conscious and considered choices rather than reacting on autopilot. Awareness also helps to break unhelpful habits.[29,30,31]

When you are at a choice point, you have only two options: to move *toward* being the vibrant version of yourself or moving *away* from this reality. It is that simple. Every choice comes back to this from how to handle the groceries to juggling a big work presentation and your little one's birthday party.

Practice making aligned choices
Get in the habit of asking yourself, "Does this move me toward being the more vibrant version of myself or does this move

me further away?" Keep that question in your back pocket for moments of uncertainty.

Next time you find yourself needing to make a decision or notice that you are about to engage in one of your unconscious, auto-pilot habits, pause. Pausing is the key. Pause and ask yourself some further clarifying questions:

- Is this decision or action aligned with my top priorities, key values, what I need and who I want to be?
- Is this decision moving me toward being the energetic and happy mom I want to be?
- What would the future vibrant me do?
- What decision or step is most aligned with my priorities, values and the life that supports me to be happy and healthy?
- Is this decision based on fear or based on my values, priorities and the life I want to create for myself and my family?
- What beliefs would the vibrant me let go of?
- How would the vibrant me treat herself? What food would she nourish her body with? How would she spend her time and energy?

The more you get in the habit of asking yourself these sorts of questions at choice points, the more likely this habit will become your new much more helpful autopiloted reaction.

Over time this method simply becomes your automatic way to make decisions. But it does take intentional practice, especially at the beginning. Become the vibrant mama of your dreams by choosing and acting from her perspective. If you do this, you will embody her so much quicker. Let her guide your decisions for you. Always ask, "What would the vibrant me do?" Make this your mantra and you'll soon see your choices aligning more and more with your higher self.

MICROSHIFTS ARE MAGICAL

Guess what? Small decisions add up to big change. Life is made up of small daily decisions, which end up shaping the people we become, the lives we lead and the impact we have on our families and wider community.

Consistent microshifts in our daily decision making can be transformative. These little choice points happen multiple times a day and can look like:

- Will you choose to get up before the kids to have ten minutes to yourself or will you stay in bed?
- Will you choose to make a superfood smoothie or stick with your typical toast for breakfast?
- Will you choose to sit outside while you drink your coffee or rush around the house with it in your hand?
- Will you choose to close your eyes and take a couple deep belly breaths or scroll social media when you need a mini break?
- Will you choose to be kind to yourself for the decisions you made in the past or will you criticize yourself for not being good enough?

Every moment you have the power to make a microshift *toward* what you want or *away* from it. Just imagine how your life would look in a year from now if each day you made even one new, tiny decision that supported you to be your best?

While you may not be proud of choices you have made in the past or even earlier today, never forget that each moment is a new opportunity to make a new choice. There are endless opportunities to move your life in your desired direction. In other words, you have the power to shape your life by the choices you make.

Microshifts build habits

Microshifts become your habits over time.

Take ten minutes to revisit the imagined future life you envisioned where you are your most vibrant. Notice in detail what this version of you is doing as you go about your ideal day. Pay attention to the specific little habits that she is doing during the morning, throughout the day and as she prepares for rest in the evening. For example, this may look like:

- She might be getting out of bed five minutes before everyone else in the house so she can get herself dressed without interruption. Her family might have the same breakfast of a fruit and veggie packed smoothie every morning, so she frees up time in the morning. She may ensure that she drinks some of the smoothie she prepares, instead of giving it all to her kids and forgetting to have breakfast herself.
- She may take a couple deep breaths to centre herself before she responds to her baby's cries.

- She may pack herself an apple, so she too has a snack to eat when her kids have theirs.
- In the evenings she might floss her teeth and get into her own pjs as she gets her little one settled into theirs. Then she may cuddle up with her little one to read a couple books.

These are simply examples of how small the new habits can be and they are all born from the practice of making intentional and value-aligned decisions. Only write down microshifts that you truly desire and that are aligned with your values and priorities. These will look differently for each and every one of us.

Next, identify which small habit you're most excited to start incorporating into your daily life. Once you have the first one built into an automatic habit, pick another one to take on. Imagine if you make one microshift into a new habit every month? In one year, you would have twelve new habits and be leaps and bounds closer to your ideal day being a reality.

A real world example of microshift power

It was one of those nights – Moss was up a few times. The kids were full of energy in the morning and I had little patience as I packed lunches and got us ready for the day. I didn't give Moss as many cuddles as he needed. I didn't give Oak the time he needed with me before driving him to daycare. Did I feel bad about that on the drive back home? Yes. But you know what? Rather than let that morning keep me down, I chose to make different decisions for the rest of the day to realign myself.

I chose to sit down and write, even though my mind was giving me excuses like 'you are too tired to write'. I chose to be kind to myself instead of berating myself for not showing up as the mom I wanted to be that morning. I chose to take myself to a yoga class even though I felt sluggish and out of sorts. I chose to pick the kids up early so I could take them to the park for a play together before dinner. I may not have made my choices that morning based on the best version of myself, but each moment in that day I was given a new opportunity to make a different choice. I had the power to shift and I harnessed that potential.

It is the small decisions and steps that we take on a daily basis that shape the person we become and create the life we live. Act as if you already are the vibrant mama that you want to be. Make as many little choices from this perspective throughout your day and watch your dream become your reality.

Consistent, mindful action is selfcare too

Think of it this way – taking consistent action that aligns with your values is a form of selfcare. It is about creating a path of least resistance to get your needs met on a regular basis.

This empowered decision making means you are showing up in your relationships, parenting, career and all aspects of your life in the way you want to. When you do that there is less guilt, regret, anger or resentment because you are operating from a place of calm instead of overwhelm. And when you treat *yourself* in alignment with your values? Whoa! That will revolutionize your relationship with yourself and your entire life.

For instance, three of my key values are clarity, simplicity and appreciation. As I go about my day, I remind myself of these values and consider how I can apply them to my interactions, work, how I respond to others and how I treat myself. I ask myself questions like:

How can I bring more simplicity to my health, career or parenting?

How can I bring more clarity to this situation?

What can I appreciate right now?

Through constant microshifts, I have developed the habit of telling myself throughout the day that I *appreciate* myself! Being kind to myself is not something that comes naturally to me, so achieving this small yet powerful shift has been incredible, and I feel amazing for it.

Through my days, I am regularly checking in to *clarify* what I am feeling and needing, and considering how I can get my needs met in the *simplest* way. I am even writing this book on it because the results have been that wonderful!

How can you bring more intention to the choices you make in your daily life?

WHAT GETS IN THE WAY OF THRIVING

Limiting beliefs, old identities, sky high expectations, and thinking you should be a "supermom" all the time (remember, she doesn't exist) can keep you stuck in making decisions that move you further away from the energetic, happy, calm mom you want to be.

Most of us aren't aware of our beliefs since they are automatic and deeply ingrained. Which is why, as we explored in Chapter 1, it is important to consider what beliefs you have learned from others and taken on as your own that might be better left in the past. Not sure what I mean? Tell me if any of these sound familiar:

Good moms always put their children first.

Good moms make sure their children are always polite and clean.

Good moms want to be with their kids all of the time. They don't need breaks from them.

Good moms don't complain.

Feeling guilty means you are a good mom.

Good moms can get their babies to nap on a schedule.

Sound familiar? There is an endless list of possible beliefs driven by societal stereotypes or cultural beliefs that may be dictating your daily decision making. Start questioning these when you notice yourself thinking you *should* act or be a certain way. Is that thought really your own or planted in your mind by an external force?

When to shed old identities and self-imposed expectations
Are there identities that you are keeping even though you have completely outgrown them? Maybe you used to stay up till sunrise regularly before becoming a mom. Maybe you are still holding onto being a night owl even though it is costing you adequate sleep, happiness and the ability to be patient with your little

ones in the morning. Maybe it's time to let go of that identity.

What expectations do you have of yourself, your partner or your little ones that are causing frustration, resentment or overwhelm? Do you expect that you can manage a full-time job, hold down the house, be with your kids 24/7 and be a "perfect" wife all times? What is this costing you? Is it helpful to let this expectation guide your choices or will that eventually lead to further burnout?

The trick to answering any of these questions is honest reflection and being aware of your key values, your top priorities and your personal needs. Focus on what matters most, say 'no thank you' to limiting factors and make intentional choices that you are proud of. With practice it will get easier and more habitual to make decisions from this place.

Take responsibility for yourself

Something else that holds many of us back from becoming content, confident and calm in motherhood is not taking responsibility for ourselves. Sounds a bit rough, I know, but hear me out.

Taking responsibility for yourself isn't about loving your current circumstance or accepting wrong doings by others – not at all.

It is about radically, completely accepting what *is* because you cannot change the past or other people's behaviour. It is about taking responsibility for how *you* choose to respond to your situation, how *you* choose to act toward others, and how *you* choose to create your future.

Taking responsibility gives you the impetus to make decisions that move you toward that vibrant future that you want where you have energy, happiness and fulfilment in your life. Surprisingly, taking full responsibility for yourself creates motivation and momentum.

In other words, practicing acceptance of what is and taking full responsibility for the choices you make and actions you take is about focusing on what you have control over – how you show up in your present and shape your future. This isn't about taking blame for or condoning what happened in the past. It is letting whatever happened in the past be because, well, it is impossible to change the past. It is infinitely more productive and uplifting to focus your efforts on how you move forward.

If you know what you want, you are clear on what is most important to you and you take full responsibility for yourself, you are unstoppable. Truly. You will have the power to create the life you want through the ability to choose wisely. And no one can take that away from you.

Learn to say no

But wait, I've saved perhaps the best revelation for last – making decisions from the place of the vibrant you and being crystal clear on your priorities, values, and needs suddenly makes saying no so much easier.

If it doesn't align with the higher you, the answer is no. Clean, simple, empowered action. How amazing is that? Better yet, this opens up more opportunity (as well as more time and energy) to say yes to the things that matter most to you and truly light you up!

Next time a request, expectation or demand is placed on you, check in with the vibrant you first before answering. Take a beat and ask:

- Does this request align with my values?
- Is it connected to my top priorities?
- Is my body energized by this opportunity?
- Does this request move me closer to the vibrant me or further away?

If it doesn't align or takes you away from who you want to be and what you want your life to be about, then it is a no. Simple, direct and finite, which is valuable because, as you are fully aware, you don't have infinite time and energy.

Remember, by saying yes to one misaligned opportunity, that yes is taking you away from other opportunities that might have brought you more aligned joy.

As always, I find examples to be enlightening, so let's run through some:

- If you agree to edit all of your co-workers' projects, you can't simultaneously be working on your own. And if you do manage to squeeze everything in, by the time you get home, you might not have much energy left for being an engaged and energetic parent as well.
- If you choose to be the primary carer for your kids without any external supports, then it is going to be bloody hard to work a full-time job, advance your career and

show up as the best mom you can be. We can do anything, but we can't do it all, all at once, all by ourselves.

Do you see how ignoring your priorities can negatively impact
your energy, your happiness, your needs and your family? Learn
to say no.

Saying no is the authentic path

Imagine if you asked your friend to go for a walk with you and
she said yes, not because she wanted to but because she felt
obligated or feared that you wouldn't like her if she said no.
During the walk she was stressed about not having time to get
caught up on her work, so she was going to have to stay up late
and not spend the evening with her family. She even felt a bit
resentful toward you, yet she had said yes, and you didn't realize
how she was feeling. Would you still want to go on this walk
with your friend? I sure wouldn't! I know I want my friends
to say yes to me when they truly want to, not because of any
yucky beliefs or expectations they might have.

What are you saying yes to, but being inauthentic, stressed
and maybe even resentful about? Be honest with yourself and
start creating boundaries by saying no. Those boundaries will
protect your authentic self and allow that authentic self to show
up more consistently. Ask yourself, are you saying yes to what
matters most to you or are you giving in out of fear, a desire
to please others or out of habit?

NOTE: It is important to mention that some people in your life
may never understand or agree with what you are choosing for

your life. They may find it really challenging that you are no longer saying yes to every request they have of you. They may not understand your new value system or dedication to prioritizing yourself. These will be hard moments but in them you still have the power to choose what is best for you and make a decision that is not driven by external factors. Remember, this is your life. There is no right or wrong choice and you are allowed to say no when it doesn't serve you. And it can be helpful to get additional support from a friend, partner or therapist to help navigate these tricky times if needed.

HER STORY:

JULIE, PEOPLE PLEASER AND MAMA OF TWO

Julie, who is 37-years-old with two boys ages 5 and 2, became overwhelmed and confused very easily. She struggled to make decisions.

HER STRUGGLE

She always worried what others would think of her. For years she said yes to everything someone asked her. Could she bring one of her beautiful cakes to a friend's baby's first birthday party? Yes. Could she help a colleague out even though she was swamped at work herself? Of course. Could she volunteer at the preschool's fair? Yes. Yes. Yes.

Julie felt busy and exhausted in her own life. Between work and family, she never felt like she could be caught up and be able to enjoy her time with her two kids. She wasn't clear on her priorities, values or needs. And she felt uncomfortable saying no to other people. So, she said yes and slowly moved herself further away from the life she wanted to be living.

HER ACTION

Once Julie got crystal clear on what she wanted her life to be about, her priorities, and her values, it suddenly became a lot easier to say yes or no to requests depending on if they aligned with what she wanted. She often said yes to the requests from her friends to go for walks even though she felt so busy, because she highly valued connection and knew that her own health was a priority. Being aware of this specific priority made walks with friends an easy yes.

It was also easier to say no to things that didn't light her up now. When her friend asked to come over for a visit with her kids on a day that Julie's kids were in daycare, she now felt strong in her decision to say no. This was her time to work on projects she was passionate about and get caught up so she didn't have to squeeze this work into time when she wanted to be with her family.

She said no to her friend, not because she doesn't care about her but because saying yes to this meant saying no to something else, specifically having the day to catch up on important work and take care of her health by going to a yoga class. She wouldn't be acting aligned with her core values of authenticity and connection since the whole time her friend was visiting, she would be preoccupied with her growing to do list. Julie also recognized that in the past when she said yes to these requests, resentment would grow, and she wouldn't act like the kind and present friend she would like to.

HER NOW

At first, Julie was nervous to say no to the requests that took her away from what was most important to her. But quickly she felt energized when she said no. She felt empowered and motivated to create the life she wanted. And when she simply explained to others why she chose to say no, they almost always respected her choice. In time she noticed that her resentment toward others lessened and she became calmer and happier with the clarity and increased time and energy to devote to her core priorities.

Clarity equips you for a life of ease

You are now equipped to make decisions more easily and these decisions will pave the way toward a motherhood (and overall life) that you can truly find joy, fulfilment and ease in. Your outer world is becoming more aligned with what you want because you are intentionally shifting your inner world – getting clear on your vision, priorities and values and making decisions from this place.

It is easier to accept or decline invites since you are now able to base your decisions off of what matters most to you, how you want to show up in your life and what it is that you need. Stay connected with what you want for your future and keep prioritizing yourself. Making choices and taking action from this place will become your go-to and you will be leaps and bounds ahead. You are arriving at where you want to be!

YOUR NEXT STEPS

....

The following are some questions to make decision making easier and move you even closer to embodying a happy, energetic and confident mama.

Better decisions

- Does this move me toward being the more vibrant version of myself or does this move me further away?
- Does this support me in moving toward the life I want to create?
- What would the future vibrant me do in this situation?
- What decision is most aligned with my priorities, values and the life I want to create for myself and my family?

Microshifts

- What tiny step can I take today to move me in the direction I want to go?
- What is one microshift I can start building into my daily life starting today?

What gets in the way

- What is getting in the way of you making your best choices?

Say no

- What do I currently find myself saying yes to that leaves you feeling drained?
- What can I start saying no to?

THINGS TO REMEMBER

Better decisions are your superpower
- What you base your decisions on shapes your life.
- Making decisions based on your current state of burnout or overwhelm will likely keep you feeling this way.
- Making intentional choices from the perspective of the future vibrant you who is aware of her values, needs and emotions will likely lead to a creating a more vibrant life one decision at a time.

Microshifts are magical
- Microshifts build habits and habits build your days, weeks and future.

What gets in the way of choices that help us thrive
- Limiting beliefs, old identities, impossible expectations and unhelpful ingrained habits can keep you stuck.
- Awareness of what gets in the way allows you to consciously choose a different path.
- Acceptance of your current reality and taking responsibility for your choices moving forward are critical to creating the future you desire.
- Clarity about your priorities, values, needs and the future you want make it easier to say no to what doesn't align with this. Start saying no to requests that don't fully support the best version of yourself.

Celebrate Being a Vibrant Mama

If you have stuck with me till the end of this book, firstly I would like to thank you for spending this time with me. The fact that you have means you are already prioritizing yourself. Congratulations! You have already achieved so much!

You are carving out a new way of living that honours yourself as much as your children, partner and others in the world.

You are taking care of yourself because you are now living more aligned with what matters most to you.

You are recognizing that caring for yourself is the best way to care for your children and to help your kids to grow up to respect, care and love themselves too.

You are moving from exhaustion, overwhelm and uncertainty to calm, contentment and confidence.

You've also made tremendous progress in so many other ways:

- You have a clear vision of what you want your life to look like.

- You know what being a vibrant mama is to you.
- You are prioritizing yourself so you can be the best mother to your children.
- You are clear on your values and use these to guide your decisions and actions.
- You are connecting with your emotions and noticing your unmet needs. With this awareness, you are finding ways to care for yourself, give yourself what you need in the moment or seeking out appropriate support from others
- You are making choices based on where you want to be – a vibrant mama, not where you currently are.
- You are on the journey from just surviving motherhood to thriving.

And by doing so, you are a role model for the mothers around you and the others to come after you. Yes, motherhood is arguably the most life changing and challenging time in our lives, but you can move through it in a way that is empowering, liberating and full of vitality. You can love and enjoy it without feeling constantly overwhelmed!

Revisit this book when you need it

My hope is that you will revisit this book any time you need a reminder on why taking care of yourself is essential for taking care of your kids. It can be helpful to come back to specific chapters as needed. Review the necessary chapter and repeat the exercises within it to refresh, realign and further integrate these skills into your daily living.

It typically takes at least three times of reading something to solidify it in your memory and doing the practical implementation is essential for the knowledge to convert into real life changes. Mothering is a tough gig, and we all need continual support and guidance throughout it. May this book be a source of support when you need it most.

Remember that the journey to being a vibrant mama is never-ending

While this book is aimed at mothers navigating life with babies and young children, the lessons and skills within it are universal to all. As your kids grow older and your roles shift, prioritizing yourself, nourishing yourself and letting go of the unnecessary are still just as essential. Who couldn't use a bit more clarity, awareness of our emotions, simple ways to meet our own needs and ease with decisions?

Becoming a vibrant mama doesn't only allow you to thrive in motherhood, have the energy to play with your kids and create a meaningful life on your terms. It also helps to make those societal pressures, norms and expectations of mothers crumble.

No longer are you at their mercy, scrambling to measure up to expectations that are unattainable and likely uninteresting to you. No longer are you falling into the mom guilt traps and selflessness that society assumes of mothers and keeps them stuck. You are centred in your own values and priorities. You are empowered to take responsibility for your health, wellbeing and future with confidence.

You have let go of the unnecessary to allow for what is most important and meaningful to have more space in your life. Through your work, creating this life in which you truly thrive, you are also creating it for your children and allowing other mothers to step into their own power. You are creating a new path for future mothers to walk as they too enter motherhood.

As a collective, we moms can change the world for ourselves, our children and other moms past, present and future. So, go forth, mama and shine in all you do!

Be the calm, content and confident vibrant mama you are!

Mother with presence.

Do meaningful work with vigour.

Build the life you desire with intention.

Be the role model for your children.

Free other mothers to live the life of their dreams.

Create the world you are proud to leave for your children, your children's children and their children's children.

I wish for you to have the clarity, nourishment and freedom to let go of what is not serving your highest self. Here is to moving forward in your life as a Vibrant Mama!

Embrace your own style of motherhood on your terms.

xx

Dr Hilary Claire

ABOUT THE AUTHOR

Dr Hilary Claire is a clinical psychologist specialized in nutritional and environmental medicine, a yoga teacher and a mom of two little boys. She helps moms move out of exhaustion, depletion and overwhelm not only because of her professional training, but because she too has lived that ups and downs of early motherhood.

We live in a world that makes motherhood so much harder than it needs to be on mamas. Dr Hilary Claire helps mothers thrive in their many, many roles by integrating proven systems of simplicity, clarity and non-negotiable selfcare into their daily lives. (Sounds impossible, right? It doesn't have to be!) She is here to guide you in achieving a happier and healthier life by taking care of mama's wellbeing first – an essential stepping stone to better family health as a whole.

When she isn't supporting moms to take optimal care of themselves, Dr Hilary Claire is helping them to give their children's brains the best start in life. She blends nutrition and environmental medicine with mindfulness, psychology and low tox living strategies to improve little ones' brain health and mama's wellbeing.

Dr Hilary Claire resides in a small coastal city in northern New South Wales, Australia. She divides her time between the beaches here and the snow of Canada, where she is originally from.

She obtained her Ph.D. in clinical psychology from the University of Wollongong after completing her Bachelor of Arts and Master's at Carleton University. Her Bachelor focused on health psychology, while her Master's degree in psychology centred on children's social and emotional development. Her Ph.D. concentrated on emotional intelligence and mindfulness in children and teens.

Dr Hilary Claire has completed courses in nutrition at Acadia University and in integrative healthcare with the MINDD Foundation. She does on-going post-graduate training in nutritional and environmental medicine with particular emphasis on brain health and children's health through the Australasian College of Nutritional and Environmental Medicine. She also continues to upskill in mindfulness, psychological therapies and yoga philosophies.

ACKNOWLEDGEMENTS

A massive thank you to Luke for having a steadfast belief in me even when I questioned if I was on the right path with my career and for dealing with the moments I fell back into the struggle as I relived stories from my past.

Oak and Moss, for all the learning and growing you have motivated me to do. Mothering is really all about the inner work. When you do the inner work, parenting comes with so much more ease.

Mom, you and Dad have always been my greatest supporters and editors since I was young. Thank you for continuing to be. Thank you for bringing your attention to detail and editing to this book too. I am so lucky to have a mom who is an incredible role model as a mother, friend and creative, but also, I am grateful for your passion for editing.

Dad, you may no longer be earthside with us, but you are still so present in my life. You were here as I typed away on this computer. I got my commitment and determination from you. Those are some of my greatest strengths. They have seen me through my Ph.D., and now this book too. I have stayed the course. Thank you for helping me do so. I do miss your editing and critical analysis skills, though. I wish I could have had your input on this book and all future books.

Emma Franklin Bell, if it were not for your guidance, support and accountability, I would likely still be sitting on several half-finished, but ever-expanding manuscripts instead of the three completed books I now have.

Laura Benn, I am grateful for the way you work your magic in editing and for your friendship. I feel so lucky to have a friend with whom we also fit so seamlessly into each other's professional lives. I look forward to a long working career together.

Thank you to Sandy Curtis and Lana Risi, for without your care of my two little boys, I could not have dedicated adequate time to see this book through in the time I did. You are like family to us and we are grateful for the kindness, calm and play that you both instil in my boys.

My deepest thanks to the friends and clients who have allowed me into their lives and shared their struggles, most private thoughts and journey with me. I am indebted to you and will always hold your stories with the utmost care.

And a final thank you to the many beaches, headlands and forests that gave me the breaks I needed, the inspiration of new ideas and got me back into my body after too much time in front of the computer screen.

FURTHER READING AND RESOURCES

Should you be interested in diving further into the topics covered in this book, here are a few books and resources I would recommend:

Emma. (2018). *The mental load: A feminist comic*. Allen & Unwin.

Harrison, K. (2020). The Postnatal Reboot. Little Yarrow. https://littleyarrow.com/the-postnatal-reboot-course/

Menkedick, S. (2020). *Ordinary insanity: Fear and the silent crisis of motherhood in America*. Random House US.

PANDAS. *Perinatal anxiety & depression Australia* https://www.panda.org.au

Serrallach, O. (2018). *The postnatal depletion cure: A complete guide to rebuilding your health and reclaiming your energy for mothers of newborns, toddlers, and young children*. Grand Central Life & Style.

Weaver, L. (2017). *Rushing woman's syndrome*. Dr Libby Online.

Weaver, L. (2019). *The invisible load*. Dr Libby Online.

REFERENCES

Chapter 1 – Release

1. Serrallach, O. (2018). *The postnatal depletion cure: A complete guide to rebuilding your health and reclaiming your energy for mothers of newborns, toddlers, and young children.* Grand Central Life & Style.

2. Harrison, K. (2020). The Postnatal Reboot. Little Yarrow. https://littleyarrow.com/the-postnatal-reboot-course/

3. Lin, S. (2018). *The Dental Diet: The Surprising Link Between Your Teeth, Real Food, and Life-Changing Natural Health.* Hay House, Inc.

4. Lin, S. (2020, Nov 14). *High sugar diets deplete the body of these four nutrients.* Facebook.

5. Masson, L. Day Three: Behavioural Issues and the Link to Food. Additive Free Summit, accessed on 12 July 2018, additivefreelifestyle.com/additive-free-lifestyle-summit-day-three/

6. Masson, L. (2018a). *ADHD.* [Conference Session]. Mental Health. Australasian College of Nutritional and Environmental Medicine. https://online.acnem.org/

7. Fallon, S & Enig, M. (1999). *Nourishing Traditions: The*

Cookbook that Challenges Politically Correct Nutrition and the Diet Dictocrats. 2nd Ed. Washington, DC: New Trends Publishing, Inc. Washington, DC.

8. Simopoulos, A P, & Salem, N. (1992). *American Journal of Clinical Nutrition,* 55:411-4 as cited in Fallon & Enig, 1999.

9. Weaver, L. (2017). *Rushing Woman's Syndrome.* Dr Libby Online.

10. Brighten, J. (2019). *Beyond the Pill: A 30-Day Program to Balance Your Hormones, Reclaim Your Body, and Reverse the Dangerous Side Effects of the Birth Control Pill.* Harper One.

11. Brighten, J. (2020). Birth Control - What Doctors Don't Say About Birth Control Effects. *Dr Brighten.* https://drbrighten.com/birth-control-what-your-doctor-didnt-tell-you/

12. Lin, S. Vitamin D Through Sun: 9 Tips to Optimize Your Levels. *Dr Steven Lin.* https://www.drstevenlin.com/optimize-vitamin-d-through-sun/

13. Cordova, A. & Alvarez-Mon, M. (1995). Behaviour of zinc in physical exercise: a special reference to immunity and fatigue. *Neuroscience and Biobehavioral Reviews,* 19(3), 439-445.

14. Grases, G., et al. (2006). Anxiety and stress among science students. Study of calcium and magnesium

alterations. *Magnesium Research,* 19(2), 102-106.

15. Golf, S.W., et al. (1998). On the significance of magnesium in extreme physical stress. *Cardiovascular Drugs and Therapy,* 2, 197-202.

16. Martínez A.C., et al. (2002). Status and metabolism of iron in elite sportsmen during a period of professional competition. *Biological Trace Element Research,* 89(3), 205-213.

17. Okamoto H, et al. (2002). Effects of stress on the urinary excretory pattern of niacin catabolites, the most reliable index of niacin status, in humans. *Journal of Nutritional Science and Vitaminology,* 48(5), 417-419.

18. Wei C., et al. (2008). Effects of psychological stress on serum iron and erythropoiesis. *International Journal of Hematology,* 88(1), 52-56.

Chapter 3 – Prioritize

19. O'Meara, C. (2013). *Changing Habits Changing Lives.* Changing Habits Pty Ltd. The Chemical Maze Pty Ltd. (2016).

20. The Chemical Maze – Complete Edition (Version 3.0) [Mobile application software]. Retrieved from http:// itunes.apple.com

21. Stratham, B. (2006). *The Chemical Maze: Your Guide to Food Additives and Cosmetic Ingredients.* Summersdale.

22. Song, E. Healthy Gut, *Thriving Child: Preventing and*

Healing Leaky Gut in Your Child [Conference Session]. The Thriving Child Summit. https://thrivingchildsummit.com

23. Song, E. Artificial Flavors, Preservatives & Dyes – Oh My! *Healthy Kids Happy Kids.* https://healthykidshappykids.com/2016/08/04/artificial-flavors-preservatives-dyes-oh-my/

24. Masson, L. (2018, July 12). *Behavioural Issues and the Link to Food* [Conference Session]. Additive Free Summit. www.additivefreelifestyle.com/additive-free-lifestyle-summit-day-three/

25. Masson, L. (2018). ADHD. [Conference Session]. Mental Health. Australasian College of Nutritional and Environmental Medicine. https://online.acnem.org/

Chapter 5 – Clarity

26. Rowsell, H. C. (2015). *Exploring the link between emotional awareness and social functioning during adolescence.* Doctor of Philosophy (Clinical Psychology) thesis, School of Psychology – Faculty of Social Sciences, University of Wollongong. http://ro.uow.edu.au/theses/4421

27. Rowsell, H. C., Ciarrochi, J., Deane, F. P., & Heaven, P. C. L. (2016). Emotion identification skill and social support during adolescence: A three-year longitudinal study. *Journal of Research on Adolescence,* 26(1), 115-125. doi.org/10.1111/jora.12175

28.	Siegel, D., & Payne-Bryson, T. (2011). *The Whole Brain Child: 12 Revolutionary Strategies to Nurture Your Child's Developing Mind, Survive Everyday Parenting Struggles, and Help Your Family Thrive.* Delacorte Press.

Chapter 6 – Thrive

29.	Ciarrochi, J., Bailey, A., & Harris, R. (2013). The 'Choice Point' Worksheet. Retrieved from actmindfully.com.au/upimages/Choice_Point.pdf

30.	Ciarrochi, J., Bailey, A., & Harris, R. (2015). *The Weight Escape.* Penguin Books.

31.	Ciarrochi, J. & Bailey, A. (2008). *A CBT-Practitioner's Guide to ACT: How to Bridge the Gap Between Cognitive Behavioral Therapy and Acceptance and Commitment Therapy.* New Harbinger Publications, Inc.: Oakland, CA.

DISCLAIMER

The information in this book, on the Dr Hilary Claire website (drhilaryclaire.com), across all social media services and within all other books, courses or products is intended as general and educational in nature. It is not personal health advice and should not be used to prevent, diagnose, or treat health problems. The contents here are for informational purposes only. It is not therapy or in replace of therapy. Always seek the guidance of a physician or other qualified healthcare provider with your questions regarding medical conditions or psychological diagnoses. You, the reader, are solely responsible for the choices you make for your health and the health of your family. You should consult a knowledgeable health practitioner to discuss what works best for your unique circumstances. All names and identifying characteristics of real people were changed to protect these individuals' privacy. Permission has been sought for use of anyone's experiences within this book.

CONNECT WITH THE AUTHOR

🌐 www.drhilaryclaire.com

📷 @drhilaryclaire

f @drhilaryclaire

Printed in Australia
AUHW021744210322
361167AU00010B/331

9 780645 256505